Teacher's Guide to
ANALYTIC PERCEPTION

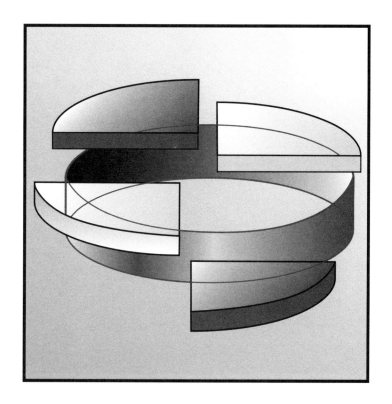

Reuven Feuerstein

IN COLLABORATION WITH

Mildred B. Hoffman

Teacher's Guide to Analytic Perception

Authorized North American publisher and distributor:
SkyLight Professional Development
2626 S. Clearbrook Dr.
Arlington Heights, IL 60005
Phone 800-348-4474, 847-290-6600
Fax 847-290-6609
info@skylightedu.com
http://www.skylightedu.com

Creative Director: Robin Fogarty
Managing Editor: Julia E. Noblitt
Consulting Editor: Meir Ben-Hur
Editors: Sabine C. Vorkoeper, Amy Wolgemuth
Graphic Designers: Bruce Leckie, Heidi Ray
Cover and Illustration Designer: David Stockman
Instrument Artist: Eytan Vig
Type Compositor: Donna Ramirez
Production Coordinator: Maggie Trinkle

©1995 by R. Feuerstein, Hadassah–Wizo–Canada Research Institute, Jerusalem
All rights reserved.
Printed in the United States of America.

ISBN 0-932935-98-2
Item number OTMS13

1542-CHG

Z Y X W V U T S R Q P O N M L K J I H G F E D
06 05 04 03 02 01 00 99   15 14 13 12 11 10 9 8 7 6 5 4

CONTENTS

INTRODUCTION 1

UNIT I 11
Cover Page 15
Page 1 22

UNIT II 29
Page 2 33
Page 3 39
Page 4 46
Page 5 52

UNIT III 59
Pages 6–7 63
Pages 8–9 70
Page 10 76

UNIT IV 81
Pages 11–12 84

UNIT V 95
Page 13 100
Page 14 102

Page 15 104
Page 16 106
Page 17 108

UNIT VI   111

Page 18 115
Page 19 118
Page 20 121

UNIT VII   123

Pages 21–22 126

UNIT VIII   131

Page 23 135
Pages 24–25 137

Teacher's Guide to Analytic Perception

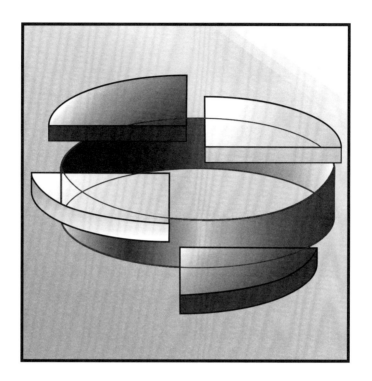

INTRODUCTION

Objectives

To teach strategies for the articulation of the field and differentiation—the division of the whole into its parts, in accordance with specific goals.

To teach strategies for integration—the synthesis of parts into a whole, according to the needs of any given moment.

To provide practice in restructuring a given field.

To encourage attitudinal and motivational changes in an individual's approach to reality by using perceptual processes to develop varied cognitive strategies.

I. CONCEPTUAL BASIS

Need for Learning to Perceive Analytically

Adaptation to the world depends on a balance between the processes of differentiation and integration. Adequate cognitive functioning requires the ability both to divide a whole into its parts (differentiation) and to join parts into a given whole (integration). Childhood is a period of mainly global perception while adolescence is normally a period of greater differentiation. It has been found, however, that some adolescents exhibit a low level of differentiation and persist in perceiving objects and events they encounter globally. The perception of differentiated parts in the external world involves behaviors that are not used spontaneously by these young people, although they may surface at times.

Goal of the Instrument

Analytic Perception uses perceptual processes to develop a variety of cognitive strategies that lead to attitudinal and motivational changes in a person's approach to reality. Individuals acquire an analytic approach that allows them to set sharp boundaries between themselves and their surroundings. Once the self is segregated from the nonself and differences between inner and outer sources of reference are recognized, the individual is able to form and then discriminately use internal references for processing information. Once an internal frame of reference is established, a person is able to structure and restructure situations on his or her own. The individual who can restructure the field is less likely to be distracted by superfluous information.

Restructuring the Field

Restructuring involves making changes in the perceptual field and going beyond the given information. It may entail one or more of the following:

1. Organizing the field in a different way.

   For example, schools are usually divided into classes based on grade and/or subject matter. At one time, sex education classes were divided according to the gender of the students. Or, a whole number can be divided into fourths, or it can be divided into sevenths.

2. Splitting up an organized field so that its parts are separate and stand out.

   For example, instead of seeing the Star of David, one sees two triangles, or a hexagon and six triangles.

3. Organizing a field that does not have a built-in structure.

   For example, projecting the square and the triangle onto an amorphous cloud of dots in Organization of Dots organized the field according to internal rules of what constitutes a square and a triangle.

The individual who can restructure the field is less likely to respond to what is salient or stands out in the situation. The cognitive restructuring of a field includes both perceptual and problem-solving dimensions that involve:

1. **Disembedding:** Locating and identifying simple elements from within a larger organized field. Concretely, disembedding may involve finding the burned out fuse in a fusebox. Abstractly, it may involve finding a subordinate set in a superordinate one (e.g., poetry as a subset of literature).

2. **Closure:** Completing a figure based on a mental picture of the object that must be identified. Examples of closure include being able to complete a sentence in which a word is missing or reading a word in which one letter is misprinted.

3. **Decentration of perspective:** The ability to recognize that a perspective from a position other than one's own differs from one's own. Being aware of the fact that a part of a whole may appear different in different contexts and from different points of view while still retaining its critical elements is a function of a decentration of perspective.

4. **Hypothesis testing:** A hypothesis is formulated and tested. "If . . . then . . ." is an important element of both structural and operational analysis.

Structural vs. Operational Analysis

Structural analysis is used to answer questions such as "What are the parts of this?" or "What is this a part of?" It involves an inventory of the parts, which are registered, labeled, summed, and related to one another. It also involves categorizing the parts in terms of the specific criteria that emerge from the whole.

An operational analysis seeks an answer to the questions. "What are the stages or steps of this process?" or "This activity is a stage or step of what process?" In an operational analysis, steps are registered, labeled, enumerated, summed, and sequenced.

The analytic process may be applied to an object or its graphic representation, to an operation, to the reasons that explain an act or event, or to a set of logical propositions. The common element in all analyses is the breaking down of a whole into its parts and the establishment of relationships between the whole and its parts as well as among the parts.

Functions and Operations Involved in the Process of Analytic Perception

The subdivision of a whole into its parts (whether the whole is concrete or abstract) requires that relationships be established between the whole and its parts and among the parts. The parts must be precisely perceived, described, identified, differentiated, discriminated, summed, and ordered.

The whole can be divided in a variety of ways, according to specific needs, and still conserve its constancy.

In addition, during the process of disembedding or seeking a part within a whole, impulsivity must be restrained and decisions deferred until the necessary information has been gathered and elaborated.

Hypothetical thinking, reflection, and inductive and deductive reasoning are important components of analysis.

II. OVERVIEW OF THE INSTRUMENT

This instrument is nonverbal and is based on the analytic perception of geometric forms. It is in keeping with one of the major objectives of Feuerstein's Instrumental Enrichment (FIE) program—that of sensitizing adolescents to stimuli that directly affect them. It helps them in the acquisition and crystallization of cognitive strategies.

The twenty-five Pages of tasks are divided into units of increasing difficulty and complexity. In the first two units, Pages 1–5, simple and complex wholes are divided into parts that are summed, and parts identical to a given standard are disembedded from the complex whole. The strategy of finding a single part within a whole is relevant to academic and vocational studies. For example, a student might be asked to find a noun in a sentence, identify the circulatory system from among other bodily systems, list the British-French wars in history, find a paragraph in a story, or identify the short leg on a wobbly chair.

In the third unit, Pages 6–10, the parts of a whole are identified, categorized, and summed. Tasks involve the recognition, registration, and inclusion of the relevant components of a whole, and the determination of their relationship to one another. Adding fractions, checking sentence structure, and reviewing the components of a cake recipe are practical applications of the principles presented in this unit.

Tasks in the fourth and fifth units, Pages 11–17, deal with the construction of wholes on the basis of identifiable parts and the closure of figures by deducing the parts that are missing and identifying them in another setting. The student moves from drawing the missing parts to completing the figures representationally. For example, a motor can be viewed as an assemblage of wholes that are composed of parts, just as the chapters of a book (each of which is a whole), are united to form the greater whole of the completed book.

In the last three units, Pages 18–25, only certain parts are disembedded from a complex array and joined together (synthesized) to a form a new whole. The previous boundaries between the various parts are eliminated in the new whole, which is the subject of attention.

For example, in health science, the heart, the arteries, the veins, and the capillaries of the human body form the circulatory system that is being studied. In auto mechanics, the ignition system, which is composed of parts that have been disembedded from the complex array of elements in a car, is being repaired.

Place of Analytic Perception the FIE Program

Analytic Perception is one of the first four instruments taught. Its tasks forge a series of strategies without which analytic perception cannot occur. However, the process is also elicited in many of the other instruments of the program, including:

Organization of Dots: Breaking down the field of dots; integrating certain dots into whole figures; disembedding a figure from among a cloud of dots; and restructuring the field.

Orientation in Space I: Spatial dimensions of orientation and direction used to describe parts, wholes, and their spatial relationship to one another.

Comparisons: Finding parts similar to given models; differentiation between parts; and discrimination of fine differences.

Categorization: A superordinate set as a whole and its subordinate subsets as the component parts; integrating separate parts into subsets or inclusive sets.

Instructions: Analyzing a set of instructions structurally and operationally to discover both its components and its sequence.

Syllogisms: Identifying an item as a member of a set and attributing to it the characteristics of all members of the set.

Representational Stencil Design: Analysis of the parts that are superimposed to form a complex design, the relationship between them, and the order of their placement.

The Teacher as a Mediator

In Analytic Perception, the mediation of transcendence and meaning assumes the utmost importance. The strategies and principles acquired in this instrument are readily applied to all areas of academic and vocational study, interpersonal relations, and daily life experiences.

The actual confrontation with the tasks will require mediation of goal-seeking, goal-setting, goal-planning, and goal-achieving behavior. Novel and complex tasks will require mediation of challenge. Mediation/regulation/control of behavior will be necessary to prevent impulsivity or, conversely, to help the student begin a task that he or she is capable of. Sharing behavior will be mediated in the course of discussions. Since the tasks themselves are constructed in order to elicit a convergent response, individualization and psychological differentiation will be mediated during discussions.

To obtain the maximum benefit from this instrument, both the student and the teacher need to know which cognitive functions the tasks address. They are:

In the input phase:

1. Precision and accuracy in gathering information and perceiving details.

2. Systematic exploratory behavior in finding the parts of the whole and their relationships.

3. Spatial and temporal elements used both as objects of analysis or as dimensions by which to describe the relationships of the parts to one another.

4. Development of verbal tools to label forms, parts, operations, and relationships, and to aid in discrimination.

5. Conservation of constancies of size, shape, quantity, and figure.

6. Seeking information from more than one source in identifying the various aspects or properties present in a situation or in the items themselves.

In the elaboration phase:

1. Perception and definition of the actual problem.

2. Selection of relevant and irrelevant information; selection or invention of relevant cues around which to organize the data.

3. Establishing or discovering a real or imaginary relationship among the various parts.

4. Spontaneous or invoked comparative behavior to differentiate and discriminate among elements.

5. Verbal mediation as an aid to the internalization of a model.

6. Hypothetical thinking and logical reasoning based on a growing need for, and increasing skills in, the pursuit of logical evidence.

7. Devising and using strategies.

In the output phase:

1. Inhibition of impulsive behavior by limiting alternatives.

2. Elimination of trial-and-error behavior by using strategies and plans.

3. Visual transport of the model form.

4. Development of verbal tools for communication or explanation of problem-solving strategies.

5. The use of quantitative and qualitative summation in the transmission of responses.

Relevance of Instrument

The student must be able to see that what he or she learns in this instrument can be applied to real-life situations and subject matter areas. Strategies and principles acquired in this instrument are relevant to any task that involves breaking a whole into its parts or merging parts into a whole, or in any area that involves following instructions or using maps, patterns, or blueprints.

In vocational areas such as construction, carpentry, dressmaking, electronics, household management, auto mechanics, and cosmetology, the need for the ability to divide a whole into its parts to determine its components and to know how to put the parts together is obvious. Less obvious, but equally important, is the need for analytic perception in all academic subjects. Whether it be the division of numbers into fractions or the analysis of the parts of an equation in math; whether it be breaking words into syllables and letters for reading and writing or breaking down a literary work to analyze its style or its characters; whether it be dividing a flower or a skeleton into its parts in science or dividing and uniting the countries of the world in geography; or whether it be solving problems in any other subject matter, the skills learned in Analytic Perception are applicable.

Teacher-student discussions are therefore particularly important in this instrument. They direct the student's attention to the process of the work rather than to its product, enhance insight, and relate the learning acquired in the Pages to both school and nonschool situations.

Use of Color

Because this instrument deals with perceptual processes, the use of color can be critical to the tasks. Color can contribute to the separation of a whole into its parts if that separation is called for in the task. If, for example, a whole is to be divided into certain parts, all of which are the same color, the use of color simplifies the task. If, however, the color separates a whole into parts that are irrelevant to the task, the color becomes a distraction, acting as a perceptual barrier that the student has to overcome.

Abridged Version

An abridged version (AV) is available for special populations on a prescriptive basis. It consists of four Pages in which principles and sample tasks are introduced and seven Pages for independent work, which are as follows: Page 3 (AV1); Page 4 (AV2); Page 8 (AV3); Page 10 (AV4); Page 17 (AV5); Page 19 (AV6); and Page 25 (AV7).

Teacher's Guide to Analytic Perception

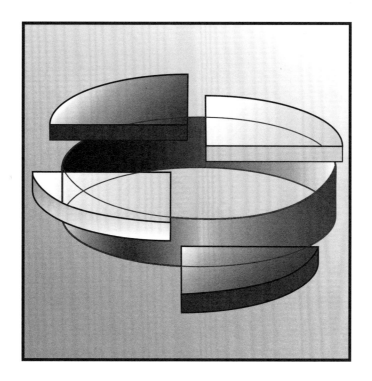

UNIT I

Objectives

To learn that a whole may be divided into its component parts.

To view each component part as a whole unto itself.

To label each part and sum the number of parts that compose the whole.

To understand that the number of parts into which a whole is divided may be arbitrary and a function of need.

Subgoal

To discriminate between the use of numbers as quantifiers and as qualifiers.

Analysis in Terms of the Cognitive Map

Content

Simple and complex geometric figures arbitrarily divided into parts.

Modality

Figural, with minimal verbal elements, and numbers used as a code.

Phase

Input

Precise and analytic perception of a whole and its parts.

Use of verbal labels for the geometric figures and of numbers as a code for the identification of parts and for communication.

Use of temporal concepts in operational analysis of a task.

Use of spatial concepts in structural analysis of a whole.

Conservation of constancy of a whole figure despite transformations that occur in its parts.

Use of a system to gather information without skipping or repeating anything.

Precision and accuracy in planning behavior.

Use of several sources of information in the differentiation of a whole into its parts.

Elaboration

Establishment of a relationship between the parts of a whole.

Comparison of tasks and their demands.

Summative behavior as an aid to reintegration of a whole.

Elimination of trial-and-error behavior through planning.

Output

Restraint of impulsivity.

Use of a code to precisely communicate information regarding both the analysis of a whole into its parts and the synthesis of parts into a whole.

Operations

Identification of parts; discrimination; enumeration; articulation of the field; inferential thinking.

Level of complexity

Generally low; moderate in figures on bottom of Page 1.

Level of abstraction

Low in tasks; high in discussion and bridging for insight.

Level of efficiency

Fairly high, except for difficulties that may be anticipated.

Anticipated difficulties due to	Methods of eliminating, bypassing, or overcoming anticipated difficulties
Lack of motivation to work on instrument when task is perceived as being too easy.	Explanation and demonstration of the usefulness of the tasks and their relevance to academic and vocational learning.
Rigidity of thought and lack of practice in moving from the concrete to the abstract.	Analysis of the elements of the concrete, formulating the principle of the task, and then generalizing to the new, more abstract situation.
Perceiving the figure globally instead of as being composed of parts that are themselves wholes.	Arousing a need to analyze a whole and differentiate its constituent parts. Using a strategy of enumeration to focus on each part in turn.
Lack of systematic work and some impulsivity so that parts are either skipped or numbered twice.	Introducing and practicing appropriate systems and strategies. Modeling systematic search.

Suggested Discussion Topics for Insight and/or Bridging

Discussion of the function and role of zip codes and area codes.

Comparison among the parts into which several students divide their day; comparison of a student's weekdays and weekends.

Use of structural and operational analysis in subject discipline and vocational areas.

Each student or small group is assigned, or selects, a task in which analysis is necessary.

Cover Page

Objectives

To arouse the need for analytic perception of an object or event.

To teach that an analysis can be both structural and operational.

To teach that every whole can be broken into its component parts.

Subgoal

To introduce some concepts that are necessary for analysis.

Vocabulary

whole	arbitrary	ellipse	component
part	quarters	analysis	structural
criteria	differentiate	operational	

Mediation

Mediation of intentionality, reciprocity, transcendence, and meaning is elicited through the interpretation of relationships between parts and between parts and wholes and the application of this understanding to other modalities and contexts.

KEY TO THE FOLLOWING TEACHER-STUDENT INTERACTION

Rationale and analysis of teacher-student interaction	Teacher questions, comments, and activities (Notes to teacher)	Anticipated student responses; examples indicating mastery
	Teacher-student interaction of development of PRINCIPLES, CONCLUSIONS, SUMMARY STATEMENTS, and INSIGHT BY BRIDGING	

Cover Page

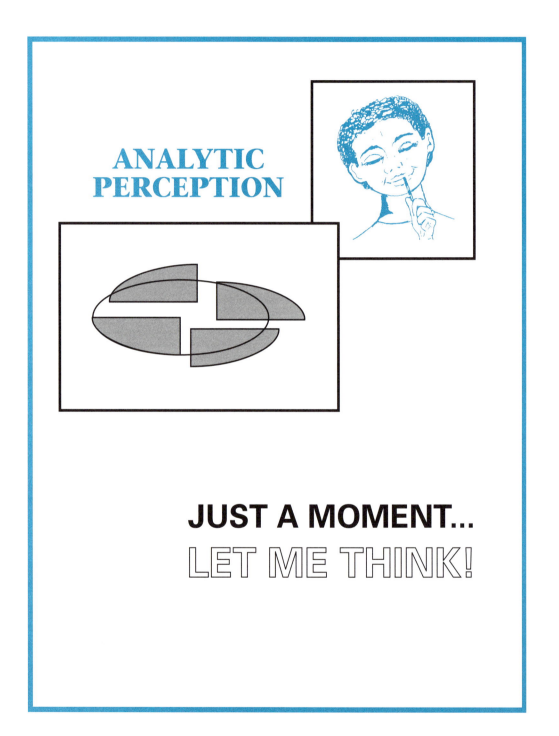

© 1995 by R. Feuerstein, Hadassah–Wizo–Canada Research Institute.

17 TEACHER'S GUIDE TO ANALYTIC PERCEPTION

MEDIATION OF:

Intentionality and reciprocity	Today we will learn that every whole can be divided into its parts.	
Focus	Please look at the symbol for the instrument. What do you see? (Draw a circle on the board.)	It is an ellipse (oval) that is divided into four equal parts (quarters).
Hypothetical thinking	Imagine that this is a cake you want to serve at home. Must it always be divided into four parts?	The number of pieces depends on the number of people we want to serve.
Developing insight	Must the parts always be equal in size?	No. Baby eats less; sister is on a diet; brother loves cake.

Meaning — **We divide a whole into its parts to answer a specific need.**

Transcendence	Using a dollar bill as an example, the following questions can be asked: Into what parts can the bill be divided? If you need change for the telephone, bus, or a parking meter, what would be required for each situation?	
Spontaneous application indicating mastery		The same bill can be divided differently each time, but it is still a dollar bill.

Meaning — **We divide a whole into its parts according to the criteria (rules) we set.**

18 TEACHER'S GUIDE TO ANALYTIC PERCEPTION

MEDIATION OF:

Selected stimuli: examples to arouse need	(Show dressmaker pattern; blueprint from carpentry shop; map of thirteen colonies and another map of same area showing states, or similar maps of England, Canada, Australia, etc.)	
Invoked comparison Reciprocity	Please look at these. What do they have in common?	They each show the way a whole thing can be broken into its parts. But it's not just parts. The parts are related in a certain way.
Probe	Can you explain?	Take that blueprint. Each piece is in a certain place in relation to the others.
Definition of structural analysis Spatial orientation	When we look at a whole and ask the question, "What are the parts of this thing and how are they related to one another?," we are dealing with a structural analysis.	
Gathering complete data	What else do we see with this pattern?	There are directions on how to put the thing together, the steps, and their order.
Definition of operational analysis Temporal orientation	When we look at a whole and ask the question, "What are the stages or steps for this activity and what is their sequence or order?," we are dealing with an operational analysis.	
Application to indicate understanding Sharing behavior	Does someone have an example of an operational analysis?	When you take apart an engine, you have to do it in a certain order; the cycles on a washing machine; adding beaten egg whites to the solids in making a cake.

TEACHER'S GUIDE TO ANALYTIC PERCEPTION

MEDIATION OF:

Insight into and expansion of a concept	In all of the examples we've had so far, concrete things have been analyzed and broken down into their parts. Do you suppose that we can analyze things we cannot touch, like ideas, time, or history?	We can divide history into its different periods. We can divide a sentence into its various parts. Time can be divided into centuries, years, seasons, months, days, etc.
Regulation of behavior		
Challenge		

Principle	**All phenomena, concrete and abstract, can be divided into their component parts by structural or operational analysis or both.**

Developing insight	Earlier we said that we divided things according to our needs. Is the division of time into night and day an arbitrary decision of ours?	Maybe not of ours, but of somebody else's. Some divisions, like light and dark, just seem to be natural.
Integration of ideas		
Probe	Is it necessary to divide day and night according to light and dark?	No, because in the summer there is more light, but the day is still only 24 hours long. In some countries, it is dark all day in the winter.

Meaning	**We may not be the ones who decide on how the whole is divided, but we must be able to recognize, identify, and label those divisions in order to be able to use them.**

Transcendence		We didn't decide how to divide the school day, but we can recognize its parts, and know that the lunch period is between certain periods. We didn't divide the week into its days, but we use those divisions to organize our lives and in all of our plans.
	Why do you think it is necessary to analyze an object or activity?	

MEDIATION OF:

Meaning	**We divide a whole—whether it is concrete (a table or dress) or abstract (time, parts of speech), an object (book) or an activity (repairing an auto)—into parts in order to help us deal with complexities.**	
Selection of stimuli and relevant criteria from among alternatives	What are some of the things to consider when we want to divide a whole?	The number of parts and their size, shape, direction, and use; the sequence, beauty, efficiency, and convenience of the division; our needs and goals.
Discussion for insight *Bridging*	How does a structural analysis help us in planning?	To know the amount and kind of material needed; to know how to lay out the material (e.g., typing, construction, gardening).
Individuation and differentiation	How does an operational analysis help us in planning?	To prevent waste (if we cut material before we measure); to prevent inefficiency (if we pave the road before the sewers are laid); to organize the task (if we answer questions before we read the chapter).
	When do we use both structural and operational analyses to complete a task?	Building a house; giving a party; filing letters; solving math problems; analyzing a chemical solution; preparing dinner.
Transfer to other areas *Transcendence*	In other subject areas, where do we analyze?	
	History: analysis of events and different societies; analysis of governments into local, county, and state levels and into executive, legislative, and judicial branches. *Geography:* analysis of countries according to natural resources, economic base, stage of development, products, altitude, climate, size, and transportation systems. *Science:* vital systems (respiratory, circulatory, etc.); structure of plants, insects, and humans.	

21 TEACHER'S GUIDE TO ANALYTIC PERCEPTION

MEDIATION OF:

Mathematics: fractions and percentages as parts of whole numbers; basic operations and functions.
Language: parts of speech; letters in the alphabet, roots of words; books divided into preface, table of contents, chapters, footnotes, bibliography, and index.
Organization of Dots: structural analysis of figures in models; synthesis of dots into figures; operational analysis in determining the strategy for solution of tasks.

Labeling the instrument

Identification: verbal

The name of this instrument is Analytic Perception. Through its tasks we will learn to divide the things we perceive into their component parts, as well as to integrate parts into an organized whole.

Application to Page

Let's look at the symbol again. Was it necessary to divide the ellipse just this way?

Fostering a sense of completion

The division of the symbol on the Cover Page is essentially arbitrary. It serves to help introduce the instrument Analytic Perception.

Page 1

Objectives

To analyze a simple or complex geometric figure into its component parts.

To recognize that every part is a whole.

To foster awareness of the necessity of labeling for identification and communication.

Subgoals

To teach the importance of systematic work.

To use summative behavior as a strategy for reintegration.

Vocabulary

simple	complex	enumeration	code
clockwise	counterclockwise	opposites	random
sum	qualitative	overlap	constancy
rhombus	counting	differentiate	quantitative
isolate			

Mediation

Mediation of feeling of competence is elicited in discussing with students the strategy for solution of tasks. Individuation and psychological differentiation is encouraged in the comparison of difficult solutions to the same task.

Page 1

Color each section a different color. Place a number in each section.

Into how many sections has the whole been divided? _____

Into how many sections has the whole been divided? __9__

Into how many sections has the whole been divided? __5__

Into how many sections has the whole been divided? __5__

KEY TO THE FOLLOWING TEACHER-STUDENT INTERACTION

Rationale and analysis of teacher-student interaction	Teacher questions, comments, and activities (Notes to teacher)	Anticipated student responses; examples indicating mastery
	Teacher-student interaction of development of PRINCIPLES, CONCLUSIONS, SUMMARY STATEMENTS, and INSIGHT BY BRIDGING	

MEDIATION OF:

Review	On the Cover Page, we were introduced to the concept of structural analysis or the division of a whole object into its parts.	
Intentionality		
Establishing relationship between Pages	On this Page we have examples of whole figures divided into parts.	
Regulation of behavior by imposed latency in defining task; reciprocity	Take a moment to look at the Page and then we'll discuss what you will be asked to do.	
(Description of task in one's own words)		Each task has a geometric figure that is divided into parts. On one side of the Page we are asked to color the parts; on the other side we are asked to number them. Then we have to write how many parts there are in each figure.

MEDIATION OF:

(Use of color) *Cause-and-effect relationship (means, end)*	Why are you being asked to color the parts?	The colors make the parts stand out from one another; they make it easier to differentiate between the parts (e.g., differently colored wires in telephone cables; different colors to designate airlines in terminals or wards in hospital).
Seeking substitute relevant to needs *Problem-solving strategies*	We have a problem. We don't have any colors. Is there an alternative? (If possible, colors should be provided to enhance the aesthetic experience. They are not necessary, however, in terms of the goals of the tasks.)	We can color the parts by using different patterns on each part, like in the example on the Page. The different patterns will let us differentiate between parts and isolate one part from another.
Meaning	**A substitute must possess a lot of the characteristics of the original that it is replacing.**	
(Use of numbers) *Deductive reasoning*	Why are we asked to number the parts?	The numbers also separate the parts. They serve as a label (e.g., police code for assault or robbery; labels for machine parts; identification for books in libraries using Dewey decimal system; license plates).
Expand the function of numbers *Discrimination and sequencing*	Is there another use for the numbers besides communication?	If they are put down in sequence, according to a system the last number will give us the total (e.g., counting-off on a field trip).
Insight *Problem-solving strategies*	Aside from colors and numbers, is there any other way we can distinguish between the parts and discuss them?	We can give them names (e.g., the blueprint for a house calls the rooms kitchen, bedroom, living room, dining room, etc.); we can give them letters such as A, B, C.

MEDIATION OF:

Comparison	Is there a difference between using the number 4 to designate a basketball player and saying "4 lbs. of apples," or saying, "I'm number 4 in line"?	The first 4 is just a label for the player. The second example gives us a quantity of apples that is four times as heavy as one pound. In the third example, 4 indicates a place in order.

Principle—Meaning — **A number may be used as a label or to indicate quantity or sequence.**

Application — In this case, the number is used to indicate a place in a sequence, and to *count* (enumerate).

Implication; critical interpretation — **We must assign the numbers systematically so that we don't number the same part twice, don't skip parts, and don't use the same number twice.**

Independent work: The only sources of difficulty stem from the lack of systematic numbering, not designating the starting point, and not using the last number as the total. (While students are working independently, draw six intersecting polygons, similar to the ellipses in the last exercise, on the board.)

Comparison of alternate systems of work *Individuation and differentiation* *Sharing behavior*	*Discussion:* I have asked five of you who had different strategies to put your solutions of the last task on the board. They are all correct, but let's compare them. (Teacher solves task in random fashion.)	The first used the system of clockwise (the direction of the numbers on the clock); the second, counterclockwise (opposite to the direction of the clock); the third, the system of opposites; the fourth, the system of dividing the parts into diagonal areas; the fifth, into three horizontal areas.
Confrontation with reality	What is wrong with this solution?	It's unorganized. You made two mistakes; you didn't fill in one part.

MEDIATION OF:

Principle—Meaning	**Systematic work, no matter what the system, is preferable to working in a random fashion.**	
Counting as a strategy Developing inferential thinking	Why do you suppose that you have been asked to sum the number of parts?	After you take something apart, you usually must put it together again. It is good idea to know how many parts there are so you don't forget any.
Transcendence	When is counting used as a strategy?	Finding the dots of the square in Organization of Dots; the number of stitches in a knitting pattern; the number of books to be sure you haven't forgotten any; number of people who are eating.
Invoked comparison Focus and selection of stimuli	What is the difference between the first two pairs of figures and the last two pairs of figures on this Page?	The first two pairs of figures are simple: a square and an octagon. The others are complex. They are whole figures composed of other whole figures.
Overcoming global perception	Into how many parts can the third figure be divided?	Three.
Inferential thinking	Would there be times when that answer would be appropriate?	If the figure were made of glass, clear plastic, or cellophane, we would be able to see the bottom figure through the top one.
	If we are asked to number the parts, as we did with the first figures, how many parts would we have? (In order to show the five parts graphically, for those with global perception, color one rhombus blue, one red, and one yellow. The overlap in which the blue and red intersect will result in purple; that between red and yellow will be orange. On the	Five.

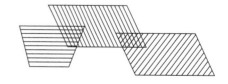

MEDIATION OF:

board, this can be demonstrated by using lines in different directions for each rhombus.)

Graphic presentation of sets and subsets

The figures can be used as examples that illustrate sets and subsets. In the first figure, we can label the center parallelogram "college sophomores," the rhombus on the left "English majors," and the parallelogram on the right "science majors." Who can describe the overlaps?

The one on the left is the subset of college sophomore English majors; the overlap on the right is college sophomore science majors.

Examples to indicate understanding

Can you think of any other examples that are illustrated by any of these tasks?

English writers, American writers, poets. Pianists, violinists, soloists.

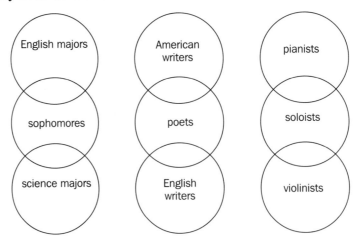

Summative behavior

What have we learned on this Page?

Meaning

Cognitive operations: verbal

To divide a whole into its parts, we must have a purpose, identify the possible divisions, and select the divisions that are relevant to the purpose.
The same whole may be divided in a number of different ways at different times to suit different needs. The parts of a whole are themselves wholes. We must be able to form a new whole by putting together (integrating) its parts. To do so, we must know both the number of parts and their relationship to one another. We must be systematic and work according to a plan.

Teacher's Guide to Analytic Perception

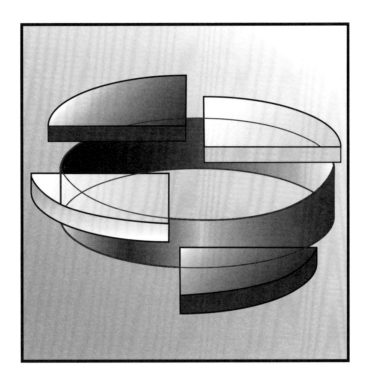

UNIT II

Objectives

To find and delineate simple and complex figures identical to given standards when they are embedded in a complex whole.

To be flexible in changing strategies to fit the changing demands of the tasks.

Pages 2–5

Analysis in Terms of the Cognitive Map

Content

Complex figures divided into various parts.

Modality

Figural, with verbal instructions.

Phase

Input

Investing sufficient time for a complete and accurate perception of the model.

Labeling the model with a universal or particular term that will aid in its recognition and identification.

Systematic search for the embedded figure.

Use of scanning as a strategy.

Representation of a change in the orientation of the figure as its position changes from frame to frame.

Conservation of the constancy of shape and size of the figure over changes in its orientation and context.

Use of various sources of information as an aid in locating the sought figure.

Use of shape and size as two characteristic and stable attributes of the sought figure.

Elaboration

Comparison of the embedded part to the given model to ascertain if it is correct.

Selection of distinctive characteristics to serve as relevant cues.

Hypothetical thinking and logic with which to prove that both the included figure (the part) and the figure that includes it (the whole) cannot be identical in size.

Interiorization of model figure and its superimposition onto a new field.

Output

Visual transport of model figure.

Restraint of impulsivity until all the information has been gathered and elaborated, hypotheses have been formulated and tested, and the responses evaluated and justified.

Operations

Articulation; discrimination; differentiation; disembedding; representation; hypothetical thinking; inferential thinking.

Level of complexity

Low for early Pages; moderate for Pages 4 and 5 because of the number of parts and their relative unfamiliarity.

Level of abstraction

Low.

Level of efficiency

High on Page 2, moderate on Page 5, and low on Pages 3 and 4.

Anticipated difficulties due to	Methods of eliminating, bypassing, or overcoming anticipated difficulties
Paying attention to the whole item globally, instead of to the characteristics of its various parts.	Analysis of the whole into its parts. Focus on a particular part and its comparison to the similar part in the model.
Temptation to designate the sought parts as those that resemble the model only superficially.	Restraint of impulsive behavior by describing the various attributes of the model, and checking the new part against the list of attributes.
Different appearance of size of object when it appears in different contexts.	Use of strategies to determine the constancy of size.
Acceptance of two forms, one of which is included in the other, as being the same size.	Use of logic and examples to overcome the problem.
Insufficient reading of instructions so that tasks are not properly completed (e.g., darkening the lines of the figures on Page 4).	Asking students to read the instructions, and to tell in their own words what they are being asked to do. After they have defined the task, they should be asked to plan the strategy for its solution.

Suggested Topics for Discussion for Insight and/or Bridging

What factors can limit the freedom of our actions? Can you think of examples of having to change your strategy because the situation changed (e.g., usually wash dishes by doing the pots last; need the pot to cook something else in, so wash it first)? Give examples from three subjects in which you were asked to find and relate to only one part of a whole. When is quantity or amount a critical factor? When do we use elimination to aid in solving problems?

Page 2

Objectives

To find one part embedded among other figures that is similar to the given model in all of its attributes except orientation.

To use two sources of information: size and shape.

Subgoal

To discriminate between similar shapes.

Vocabulary

square	hexagon	circle	particular
stable	relevant	triangle	diamond
universal	constancy	differentiate	segment
cue			

Mediation

Mediation of change and control of behavior is needed for students to invest sufficient time to investigate the tasks. Sharing behavior is mediated through the discussion of strategies and examples of transcendent applications.

Page 2

In the far left frame of each row is a part that is hidden in each of the complete designs in that row. Locate the part in each design and color it. In the design, the part may appear in an orientation different from that of the model.

© 1995 R. Feuerstein, HWCRI, Jerusalem, Analytic Perception

KEY TO THE FOLLOWING TEACHER-STUDENT INTERACTION

Rationale and analysis of teacher-student interaction	Teacher questions, comments, and activities (Notes to teacher)	Anticipated student responses; examples indicating mastery
	Teacher-student interaction of development of PRINCIPLES, CONCLUSIONS, SUMMARY STATEMENTS, and INSIGHT BY BRIDGING	

MEDIATION OF:

Definition of problem; intentionality by anticipation	What do we have to do in these exercises?	The instructions say that we must find a part that looks like the model in shape and size.
Conclusion	**We are bound by two factors at the same time.**	
Generalization		Like in Organization of Dots.
More precise definition of task; spatial orientation	Will the part always be in the same position and direction as that of the model?	No. The instructions say that it can appear in a different orientation.
Principle—Meaning	**The object is constant in its form and size despite changes in its orientation. When critical attributes of an object are conserved, the object remains the same object.**	
Application Transcendence		A tomato is the same even when it is sliced for a salad. A word is spelled the same way even when it is in a different sentence.
Planning and sharing behavior; sequencing perception; labeling; interiorization; visual transport; systematic search; comparison to model; completion of task	How shall we work? What do you suggest as a strategy?	1. Look at the model. 2. Label it. 3. Try to close our eyes and see it. 4. Look at the figures in the row slowly and systematically.

MEDIATION OF:

		5. Check it against the model when we think we have found it.
		6. Color it.
		7. Move to the next figure.
Response: verbal; use of labels to aid in search	What are we looking for in the first task? second task? third task?	Square. Triangle. Hexagon.
Use of relevant cue *Need for precision on input level*	Is the word triangle enough to help you look for it?	No, because it doesn't differentiate enough between triangles. We have to know that it has a right angle.
Overcoming irrelevant information	Do the colored lines help us find the triangle?	No, because the triangle is not completely drawn with colored lines.
Meaning	**A universal and precise label makes differentiation easier.**	
	Independent work: Row 2 presents difficulties since the change in orientation includes a flip-over of the triangle so that it appears as a mirror image. There is also an optical illusion of a difference in the size of the triangle when it appears alone, among a group of other figures, or contrasted with a larger or smaller version of the same shape.	
Insight	*Discussion:* What presented a problem?	There were similar forms, but the sizes were different.
Strategies	As I walked around, I saw some interesting strategies. Will you share them with us?	I put a little pencil mark in all the parts I looked at that were not like the model to show that I had already looked at that part.

MEDIATION OF:

Interpretation to student of meaning of act	That was an excellent strategy and a good habit to develop. That way you can be sure that you have not skipped over any parts, and can eliminate the parts that are not relevant.	
Feeling of competence		
	Are there any other ways to be sure that you have not skipped a part?	Working systematically. From left to right. From top to bottom.
Feedback	How can we be sure that we have completed the task?	We can read the instructions again to see if we did what was required. We can check the part we found against the model to be sure it's the right shape and size. We can go over the Page again to see if all the work is completed.
Fostering a sense of completion		

Conclusion	**If our task is to match a single item to a model, it is completed as soon as we have found an item similar to the model in all of its critical attributes.**

Examples of application	When are we asked to match a single item?	Looking up a word in the dictionary; finding a map of a specific country in the atlas; matching a lost button; finding a specific face in a crowd.
Transcendence		
Inferential thinking	How will the lack of universal labels affect our work?	A precise label makes differentiation easier.
Comparison to previous Pages	You remember that in the previous Page we said that the whole could be divided in any number of different ways. You can see a good example of that on these Pages.	In each row, the same figure is repeated five times. Each time it is divided into parts that are different in number and shape. The only thing the five have in common, aside from outside shape and size, is one part that is the same as the model in shape and size.

MEDIATION OF:

Discussion for insight — Can you think of examples when the outside form stays the same and one element is constant but the other components change?

A meal is the structure. What we eat at a meal is different from meal to meal, but we always drink milk.

A TV series is the form. The situation changes from program to program, but the characters are the same.

Summary — What did we learn on this Page?

Reciprocity — **We learned to define the object of our search precisely, to devise a strategy for the search, and to make the object stand out from many other parts by coloring it.**

Transcendence — *Examples:* Underlining the verb in a sentence; picking the correct answer from among multiple choices; identifying the capital on a map; finding the correct change for a bus ride; picking out your own folder from among those of other members of the class.

Page 3

Objectives

To find one or more parts identical to the model in a complex whole.

To find a strategy for checking work in the absence of immediate feedback.

To use hypothetical thinking and logical evidence for the solution of problems.

Subgoals

To discriminate fine differences.

To analyze a part into its component parts.

Vocabulary

fine discrimination   inner   interpretation   outer

Mediation

Mediation of goal-setting, goal-planning, and goal-achieving behavior is necessary on this Page. Regulation of behavior and awareness of change are necessary to attend to and determine fine differences between the given models and the content of each task.

Page 3 (AV 1)

KEY TO THE FOLLOWING TEACHER-STUDENT INTERACTION

Rationale and analysis of teacher-student interaction	Teacher questions, comments, and activities (Notes to teacher)	Anticipated student responses; examples indicating mastery
	Teacher-student interaction for development of PRINCIPLES, CONCLUSIONS, SUMMARY STATEMENTS, and INSIGHT BY BRIDGING	

MEDIATION OF:

Intentionality	Is this Page similar to the previous Pages?	Yes. We have to find a part that is the same size and shape as the model.
Comparison		
Anticipated intention		No. The shape appears more than once. There is more than one shape to find in some of the exercises. And we have to disregard the fact that some lines are colored because they are not always the same.
Reciprocity		
Perception of feelings	Will it be harder or easier? Why?	It will be harder because the shapes are complex and the differences between them are finer. Before, we could stop as soon as we found the part. Now, we have to check all the parts to be sure that we have found them all.
Identification and description	(Verbal mediation is increasingly difficult because of the irregularity of the forms. It becomes necessary to label on the basis of resemblance to known objects, or to provide a frame of reference.)	It will be harder because there is a new model for each task, and some of the tasks have two models, so there are sixteen models to look at, label, internalize, etc., instead of only three.

MEDIATION OF:

Setting a strategy	How do you suggest we work?	Look at the model very carefully and label it; carry it to the task in our imagination; compare what we find to the model.
Systematic exploration		
Definition of model	In the first exercise, what are we looking for?	Something that looks like an arrowhead, or a fighter plane, or a pointed nose.
Identification		
Conclusion—Meaning	**When a part appears more than once, we must look at every part of the whole carefully. We cannot be content with finding only a single match.**	
Systematic work	How will we be sure that we haven't overlooked anything?	We can mark each of the parts we look at. If the part is similar to the model we can write a number in it. If it is not, we can check it off.
Competence		
Review of previous strategy	A good idea. When did we use numbers as a strategy before?	On the Cover Page and Page 1 to sum the number of parts.
Conclusion	**When there is no immediate feedback, we must devise a way to check our work. We can use previous techniques if they are appropriate. If they are not, we must find new ways.**	
Definition of new problems: implied comparison and evaluation by hypothetical thought	Look at the last row on Page 3. Are there any new difficulties we can anticipate?	We must find two different models, each of which appears several times. We must find a way to designate each of the models as we find them. We can't just number and check. If we do, we'll get confused as to which number belongs to which part.

MEDIATION OF:

Individuation and psychological differentiation; exploration of alternative strategies for overcoming difficulties that can be anticipated; sharing behavior

Do you have any suggestions?

1. We can use two different colors, one for each model, and color each part that is similar to the model with the appropriate color. Then we can count the number of times each color appears.
2. We can make a tally sheet with a column for each of the models and one for the parts that don't belong to either. We can start from the upper left corner, and mark off each part as to where it belongs. We can add up each column and write the sums in the proper place.
3. We can use Arabic numerals for one model and Roman numerals for the other. We can use a red pencil for writing the numbers of one model and a blue one for writing the numbers of the other. We can use letters for one model and numbers for the other.

Critical interpretation of strategies

Which of the suggestions is the best?

Using Arabic and Roman numerals. We are able to see at a glance which parts we selected. We can also use the last number to arrive at the sum of each of the parts.

Independent work: Task 1, Row 2: The upper and lower sides of the figure at the end are narrower than those of the model. Only three parts are similar to the model.

Need for logical evidence

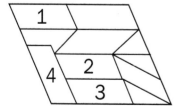

Task 2, Row 2: Four parts. Hypothetical thinking and logic eliminate one of the two choices in the upper part of the frame. Since they are two different sizes, logically only one of them can be correct. If the upper left is correct, the upper right cannot be, since the latter is larger than the former.

MEDIATION OF:

Hypothetical thinking and logical evidence

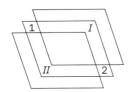

Summation

Insight

Critical interpretation

Transcendence

Task 2, Row 3: The answer is two and two. Since an object that contains another one must be larger than the object it contains, only one of each pair of the L-shaped figures is correct.

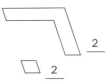

Discussion: I think you will all agree that this Page was far more difficult than we expected. Can somebody tell us why there were problems?

We had to break up the part into its component parts and look at tiny differences in size and length. Some problems could be solved using logic. If one figure is larger than another, one of them has to be wrong. If something is inside something else, the thing inside must be smaller than the thing it is enclosed in. (A foot must be smaller than a shoe; an item must be smaller than a box it is put in.)

Probe

Comparison

Earlier, you anticipated that having two models in each task would be a source of difficulty. Nobody has mentioned this yet. Why?

Meaning

An increased number of parts makes a task take longer to finish. It does not necessarily make it more difficult.

Example: A page full of different addition problems takes longer to do than one with just a few problems, but it is not necessarily harder.

What did we learn on these Pages?

MEDIATION OF:

Summary

Fostering a sense of completion

A whole may contain a number of identical parts. (A whole number may be composed of a number of equal fractions.)
It is necessary to break a part into its component parts in order to find fine differences.
It is necessary to invest as much in checking one's solution as in arriving at the response originally. (Check multiplication by division, addition by subtraction.)
It is possible to be sure we have not skipped anything by adding the number of parts that are similar to each model, and the number of parts that are similar to neither. The sum should equal the total number of parts into which the whole has been divided. (Add the amount I spent to the amount I have left and I should have the amount of money I started out with.)

Transcendence

Topics for discussion:
Limiting your options: You can go to a movie or watch television. What will limit your choice? What will affect your decision?
Planning a complex task: You are in charge of ordering supplies for a trip. There are no stores where you are going so you must bring everything with you. What are some factors you must consider if you are in charge of planning meals? How can you be sure you haven't skipped anything (e.g., number of people, length of stay, climate, transportation, activities)?

Page 4

Objective

To isolate and identify a number of parts embedded in a complex drawing.

Subgoal

To indicate mastery.

Vocabulary

framework	center	rectangle	side
methodical	middle	parallel	corner

Mediation

Mediation of challenge is elicited by this novel and complex task. Mediation of a feeling of competence may be necessary in interpreting to the students the meaning of what they are doing.

KEY TO THE FOLLOWING TEACHER-STUDENT INTERACTION

Rationale and analysis of teacher-student interaction	Teacher questions, comments, and activities (Notes to teacher)	Anticipated student responses; examples indicating mastery
	Teacher-student interaction of development of PRINCIPLES, CONCLUSIONS, SUMMARY STATEMENTS, and INSIGHT BY BRIDGING	

Page 4 (AV 2)

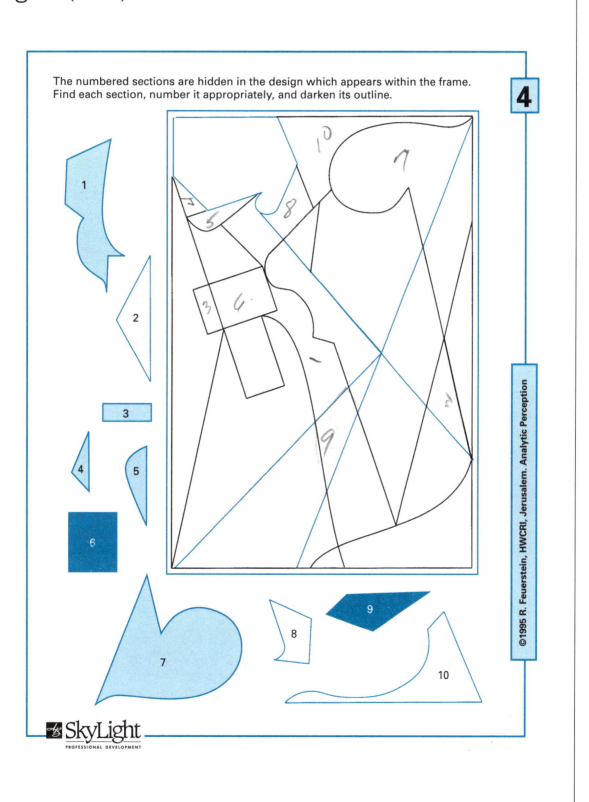

MEDIATION OF:		
Anticipated intention; definition of problem	How many parts do we have to find?	Ten.
Reciprocity	How do you know?	I counted them. I read the last number.

If all items are numbered consecutively, the highest number indicates the total number of items.

Exploration of alternate strategies for search Individuation and differentiation	Is there only one way to work?	1. We can start with part #1 and go through the whole page until we have found a part that has the same shape and size and then move on to #2. It will mean going over all of the figures each time. 2. We can start with the parts in the frame and match a piece of it at a time with the numbered forms.
Feeling of competence	Why is that not as efficient?	There are more parts in the drawing than we have to find, so it would waste time to look for a match for a piece that has none.
Individuation and sharing behavior	Is there another way?	Since each part appears only once, we can stop looking as soon as we have found its match.
Systematic exploration		Before we start, we can study all ten pieces. We can look for the irregular shapes (1—ribbon; 7—a "tuba"). Then we can start looking for #1 systematically. If we happen across another part that resembles what we remember seeing, we check it against the model, mark it off, and continue our search in sequence.

MEDIATION OF:

Precise observation

Assuming responsibility

Internalization of forms by visual transport or verbal mediation (systematic search)

Comparison to model

Hypothetical thought and logical evidence

Meaning

Application

Transcendence

Let us review how we must work.

1. We can use the same strategy we used in the other Pages to decide what we are looking for.
2. We must select a starting point and work our way systematically across (or up and down) the Page to be sure we cover all the parts.
3. Before we write the number into a part that matches, we must check the model to be sure it has the same shape and size (the orientation will differ).
4. If the model is very tiny, there is no point in looking for it in the large spaces. If the model has curved lines, there is no point in looking for it among the straight lines.

We can save time and effort by using cues and eliminating from consideration those parts that are logically impossible.

The sum of a three-place addition problem must have at least three places. If Mary and Susan are always together, and Mary is not at school, Susan isn't there either.

5. After we have found a match, we must check off that part so that we don't look for it again.
6. After we have finished, we check our work to be sure that we have followed the instructions and found a match for all the items.

MEDIATION OF:

Self-criticism	*Independent work:* (Students usually forget to darken the outline of each part that resembles a model. They should be referred to the instructions. They may also forget to mark off what has already been used, thus indicating the need for further practice.)	
Summation: comparison; analysis; perception of feeling	Was this Page difficult?	Yes, because of the number of pieces we had to find. No, because we only had to look at two factors (size and shape) for each piece.
Discussion for insight	We've talked a lot about systematic search and systematic work. Let's summarize what we know about them.	
Comparison of concepts; part-whole relationship	Is systematic search the same as systematic work?	Systematic search is only one kind of systematic work.
Intentionality and meaning	**Systematic search requires:** **Describing the object of search in terms of all its attributes.** **Narrowing the field of the search.** **Planning a strategy, including the sets to be followed.** **Hypothetical thinking and checking the hypotheses (if, then).** **Checking to be sure that what you have found is what you were looking for.**	
Transcendence	*Examples:* Looking for lost reading glasses, keys, or books by asking oneself where they were last used? (What was I wearing? etc.); looking for a number in the Yellow Pages or a word in the dictionary by precisely defining the object of the search.	

MEDIATION OF:

Systematic work	What is systematic work?	
	To work systematically is to work according to a method or a plan in a sequence. **In making a plan for systematic work, one must set priorities and order them from the most to the least important.**	
Association and applications	*Examples of activities using systematic work:* Steps in sewing a dress; building a model; working on a puzzle; washing dishes; greasing a car; painting a building; threading a film projector; using a public telephone or a vending machine.	
Setting priorities *Probe for understanding of concept* *Transcendence*	What are some examples of what we mean by setting priorities? (What is most important?)	Shopping for essentials before using balance of money for treats. Learning a prerequisite for a subject before learning the subject itself. Doing the thing that takes the most time first. Doing what is most difficult first, while one is still fresh. Doing the easiest thing first to get it out of the way and feel a sense of accomplishment.
Focusing	What is irrelevant information?	Irrelevant information is information that doesn't help us with the task. In this case, the color is irrelevant information.
	Irrelevant information is information that does not help in solving a problem. It is information we ignore. When we try to solve a problem, we should only use the relevant information.	

Page 5

Objectives

To analyze the source of errors through comparison.

To discriminate between two similar items.

Subgoal

To develop the ability to be self-critical by encouraging objectivity into an investigation of errors.

Vocabulary

if   check   audit   format

Mediation

An awareness of change must be mediated so students recognize the difference between the model figures and the erroneous figures inside the frame. Individuation and psychological differentiation are mediated in a comparison of different strategies and divergent responses.

KEY TO THE FOLLOWING TEACHER-STUDENT INTERACTION

Rationale and analysis of teacher-student interaction	Teacher questions, comments, and activities (Notes to teacher)	Anticipated student responses; examples indicating mastery
	Teacher-student interaction of development of PRINCIPLES, CONCLUSIONS, SUMMARY STATEMENTS, and INSIGHT BY BRIDGING	

Page 5

Correct the errors.
The numbered parts which appear outside of the frame are hidden within the design. After you find them, see that they are numbered correctly. Cross out those numbers which are incorrectly printed on the sections within the design.

MEDIATION OF:		
Insight into source of errors	How do errors occur?	Not following instructions (e.g., explosion in chemistry lab).
Anticipated intentionality		Not being precise in definition of size and form (e.g., cutting lumber too short).
Reciprocity		Not being systematic (e.g., forgetting to put salt in soup).
		Not preparing a total plan before starting to work (e.g., Organization of Dots).
Hypothetical thinking	**If we did not read the instructions on this Page, what error might we make?**	We would be tempted to do exactly what we did on Page 4, since the format is the same.
Definition of task; erroneous decoding; deductive reasoning; critical interpretation	**What are we supposed to do on this Page?**	We are supposed to find the ten parts outside of the frame in the drawing, and cross out the numbers that are written in the parts in the drawing.
	Where did you get that information?	The instructions say "Cross out those numbers which are . . . "
Inference	What can we infer from the word "those"?	Not all the printed numbers are wrong. Some are right, too.
Exploring implications	Is there another way to say the same thing a little clearer?	"Cross out the numbers if they are wrong."
Conclusion	**We must read instructions carefully and look for the key words.**	
Translation of written instruction into an act; problem-solving strategies	How do you suggest we work?	Like we did on Page 4. If it turns out that the model figure is the same as the one with the printed number, leave the number. If not, cross it out.

MEDIATION OF:

Evaluating the plan	Do you all agree that that is the most efficient way to work?	No, because we are ignoring all the work somebody else did before. (Similar to an auditor who, instead of checking the bookkeeper's work, does it all again.)
Feeling of competence		
Furthering goals of program	I have another objection. Remember that the objective of these tasks is not merely to get the correct answer. We are learning a strategy for checking one's work here.	
Meaning		
Seeking an alternative strategy	Is there another suggestion?	Start with #1 inside the frame and compare it with #1 outside of the frame. If it is OK, leave the printed number. If it is not, look for the correct part.
Problem-solving strategies		
	Do you all agree that that is the most efficient way to work?	No, because we have to take time to find #1 inside the frame, too.

Conclusion

Feeling of competence

Since the numbered parts inside of the frame are not numbered consecutively and those outside of the frame are, it is most efficient to work systematically, starting with the first numbered part we encounter. It is #7. We look at part #7 outside of the frame and see that the numbered part is not correct. We cross out the number and look for #7 within the frame. Then we cross out the part outside the frame to indicate that we have found it. Next, we look at #5 inside the frame, and repeat the process. We then move on to #6, which is the next numbered part we encounter in our systematic search, and so on, until the task is completed.

Transcendence

Example: If we have a list of words that are spelled incorrectly, we start with the list. Since the dictionary is arranged alphabetically, it is far easier to find the word than to thumb through the dictionary, word by word, until we find the one we need to correct.

MEDIATION OF:

Perception as a function of context or sequence

Confrontation with reality

Discussion after independent work: When I worked on this task, I had problems finding the correct #7. Did anybody else have a similar difficulty? What caused the problem?

#7 looks much bigger inside the frame than it does outside. It is the same size, though. I measured it.

I think it looks larger in the frame because it is next to very small parts.

(For example, the appearance of furniture in a very small room, as opposed to the same furniture in a large room.)

Our perception is affected by factors of context, sequence, color, and relationships.

Transcendence

Examples: A room seems dark when we come in from the sunlight; tepid water seems boiling hot if we pour it on our frozen hands; a noise seems very loud if we are in a very quiet room.

Investigating the nature of the errors

Comparative behavior

What was common among the errors?

Only one part of the part was usually wrong. The errors were usually caused by size and angles. These changed the shape of the figures in some cases.

(Some classes may be asked to chart or list the similarities and differences between the model part and the numbered part in the frame. The errors should be described precisely, in terms of shape, size, direction, angles, and orientation.)

Additional sources of errors

Precision

Can we add any other reasons to our list of sources of errors?

It seems that whoever did this Page was in too much of a hurry. He or she was satisfied with what was nearly right and didn't pay attention to details.

TEACHER'S GUIDE TO ANALYTIC PERCEPTION

MEDIATION OF:

Conclusion

It is always wise to check somebody else's work.

Examples: Counting our change before we leave the cashier; looking over a graded test to be sure that it is correctly marked.

Making a mistake is human. Checks and balances are therefore included in most systems.

Examples: Checklists for pilots and astronauts; countersignatures on checks.

Summary of unit

What did we learn from the
last Page and this one?

The same whole can be analyzed and divided into its different parts in different ways.
By clearly and precisely defining a part, it is possible to localize it in a complex whole and isolate it.
In seeking a particular part within a whole, it is necessary to consider many factors at the same time.
The process of analysis must be carried out systematically.

Teacher's Guide to Analytic Perception

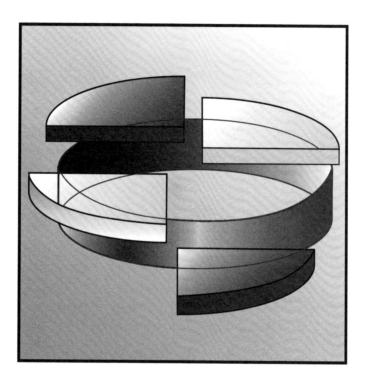

UNIT III

Objectives

To analyze a whole by the identification, categorization, and summation of its parts.

To combine synthesis with analysis in determining the specific elements that can be integrated into the whole.

To teach strategies for the cognition, registration, and inclusion of the relevant components of a whole.

Subgoal

To learn various methods for correcting errors and their appropriate application.

Pages 6–10

Analysis in Terms of the Cognitive Map

Content

Figures divided into parts and parts to be integrated into figures.

Modality

Figural.

Phase

Input

Precise perception of form, size, color, and orientation of parts.

Systematic exploration of the elements in each frame.

Use of labels that precisely denote the part and mediate in seeking it.

Simultaneous use of shape, size, color, and number in definition of parts.

Conservation of constancy of part despite changes in its orientation.

Elaboration

Spontaneous comparison to model.

Establishment of relationship between parts, and between the parts and the model.

Categorization of parts according to their shapes and colors.

Visual transport of parts to the model.

Output

Precision and accuracy in communicating response.

Restraint of impulsivity.

Operations

Articulation of field; segregation; discrimination; differentiation; categorization; integration; inferential thinking; deductive and inductive thinking.

Level of complexity

Medium to high in tasks with many unfamiliar parts.

Level of abstraction

Low in task, high in application.

Level of efficiency

High at start of unit, low for last Page of unit.

Anticipated difficulties due to	Methods of eliminating, bypassing, or overcoming anticipated difficulties
Difficulty in labeling or internalizing irregularly shaped figures.	Selection of a salient part of the whole to serve as a relevant cue for locating it.
Blocking when faced with extremely complex tasks.	Analysis of a complex whole into manageable parts. Introduction of strategies of summation, categorization, or elimination.
Strategies that are no longer effective in differentiating or integrating.	Changing the strategy to meet the demands of the changing situation.
Solution by elimination or matching on a one-to-one basis.	Reduction or matching should be discouraged in an effort to raise the level to one of categorization.

Suggested Topics for Discussion for Insight and/or Bridging

Sequence as a critical element in putting parts together.

Categorizing in our daily life (e.g., making a grocery list or doing the laundry).

What qualifiers (subsets) make it easier to identify or to find your friend at the movies? the mother of the bride? the subject of your report in the library?

Twenty Questions as an example of identifying an object or person by a statement of its/his or her attributes.

Errors of omission and commission in interpersonal relations.

Pages 6–7

NOTE: These two Pages are taught together.

Objectives

To analyze a whole using the parameters of form, number, size, and color.

To be aware that a whole is a function of its parts, but it is more than the sum of its parts.

Vocabulary

rectangle	category of class	synthesis
square	salient	element
equilateral triangle		

Mediation

Mediation for intentionality, reciprocity, transcendence, and meaning are necessary in confronting the tasks of a new unit. Sharing behavior is encouraged in comparing strategies and expression.

KEY TO THE FOLLOWING TEACHER-STUDENT INTERACTION

Rationale and analysis of teacher-student interaction	Teacher questions, comments, and activities (Notes to teacher)	Anticipated student responses; examples indicating mastery
	Teacher-student interaction of development of PRINCIPLES, CONCLUSIONS, SUMMARY STATEMENTS, and INSIGHT BY BRIDGING	

Page 6

In each of the following exercises you are given a model. Choose the box which contains all the parts that make up that design and write its number in the circle provided.

6

Page 7

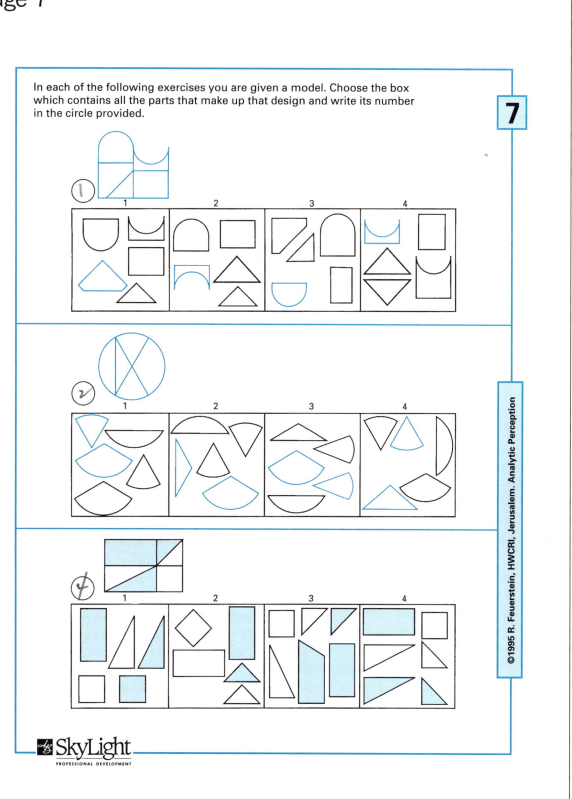

MEDIATION OF:

Review and comparison	This is a new unit. How does it differ from the last one?	Before we were given a whole divided into parts and had to identify either one or a few of its parts.
Definition of problem; intentionality and reciprocity		Here, we must identify all the parts that make up the whole.
Understanding nature of task		*Examples:* Instead of finding just one screwdriver in an electrician's kit, we have to find all the parts that make up the kit. Instead of finding just the verb in the sentence, we have to identify all the words that are included in it.
Transcendence		
Gathering the information	What are we given in the first task?	A model that has five parts.
Directing attention	Will just the number of parts help us to find the frame that contains the parts of the model?	No, because frames 1, 2, and 4 each have five parts. But it will help us to eliminate frame 3. It only has four parts so we can cross off that possibility.
Problem-solving strategies	**We can narrow the field of search by elimination.**	
Seeking precise information	What will help us in our search?	There are two of one shape and three of another, but that's not much help because both frames 2 and 4 have two of one shape and three of another.
Probe; precision	Two of what and three of what?	Two rectangles and three squares.

MEDIATION OF:		
Labeling by categories using two sources of information: number, figure		So we write #2 in the circle.
Comparison and evaluation; perception of feeling	Why is the second task hard?	Because all the frames have four parts.
Principle	**A characteristic common to many objects does not differentiate between them.**	
	Example: One cannot ask to see "a pair of shoes" in a shoe store.	
Seeking point of reference *Identification and description*	Is there some way we can describe what we have been given?	There is no name to describe some of the figures. We can say one big and one small equilateral triangle and two identical parts that are not triangles.
Conclusion	**Whenever there are forms that are easily labeled, the labels should be used in their categorization.** **When the form has no universal label and is complex, its salient characteristic or its resemblance to a familiar object can serve as a basis for its categorization.**	
	Independent work: (Task-bound students may attempt to solve the tasks by one-to-one matching, similar to that used in previous tasks. An effort should be made to raise the level of the task to one in which categorization and summation are the critical factors in its solution.)	
Individuation and differentiation *Sharing*	*Discussion:* What strategies did you use?	We can work by elimination. If there is not the same number of parts in the frame as there is in the model, we can ignore that frame.

MEDIATION OF:

Insight into divergent strategies and their evaluation		If there is more than one color, we can use color as a basis for elimination (e.g, Page 7, ex. 3: not enough dark pieces in frame 2, wrong shape of dark pieces in frame 3.)
Principle	**Elimination will tell you what is not appropriate; it does not tell you what is.**	
		We can match each part in the frame to each part in the model.
Problem-solving strategies	**Matching may be effective if there are only a few items to match or from which to choose.** **It is inefficient and time consuming when there are many parts.**	
		We can organize the parts by shape and use number, size, and color to describe the shapes.
Conclusion Cognitive operation: verbal	**The organization of parts that share characteristics on the basis of their commonality is called categorization or classification.**	
		Categorization is the most effective way to organize the parts of a whole.
Insight	In these tasks we are dealing with synthesis, the opposite of analysis. It means putting things together.	When I look at these tasks, they remind me of parts of a pattern that I must lay out on a piece of material for cutting without any waste.

MEDIATION OF:

Feeling of competence *Interpreting to the student the meaning of his or her response*	That's a very interesting comment. The principle of economy would determine the synthesis. You would have the whole as a sum of its parts (e.g., like in math: 3+5+2=10, 5+2+3=10, 2+3+5=10, 2+5+3=10).	
Expansion of concept	Here, however, we can see the whole as more than the sum of its parts. Let me give you an example:	
Transcendence	If we have flour, eggs, milk, salt, shortening, baking powder, and sugar, what can we make?	Cake, pancakes, pudding, muffins, cookies.
	What will make the difference?	How you put them together (order), the proportion of one ingredient to the other (quantity), and whether you bake or fry the mixture (process).
Principle	**The whole depends on the parts and their relationship to one another.**	
Anticipation *Fostering a sense of completion*	This is just the beginning of the unit. There will be more opportunities to discuss the breakdown of a whole into its parts (analysis) and putting the parts together to form a new whole (synthesis).	

Pages 8–9

NOTE: These two Pages are taught together.

Objectives

To discriminate between wholes and their components.

To identify the components of a specific whole.

Subgoal

To select relevant cues.

Vocabulary

components	mixture	embedded	keystone
exception	compound	unique	

Mediation

Mediation for goal-setting, goal-planning, and goal-achieving behavior is required in these Pages, which include a number of different tasks. Regulation of behavior is necessary for sufficient investment of time to perceive cues and discriminate among available responses. Mediation for individuation is encouraged in contrasting different strategies.

KEY TO THE FOLLOWING TEACHER-STUDENT INTERACTION

Rationale and analysis of teacher-student interaction	Teacher questions, comments, and activities (Notes to teacher)	Anticipated student responses; examples indicating mastery
	Teacher-student interaction of development of PRINCIPLES, CONCLUSIONS, SUMMARY STATEMENTS, and INSIGHT BY BRIDGING	

Page 8 (AV 3)

In the large frame you have several models. For each model, choose the box which contains all the parts that make up that design and write its number in the space provided.

Page 9

9

In the large frame you have several models. For each model, choose the box which contains all the parts that make up that design and write its number in the space provided.

MEDIATION OF:

Intentionality and reciprocity *Definition of task*	What are we being asked to do?	There are six different wholes on the top of the Page, and six frames with parts on the bottom of the Page. We are supposed to find which components belong to which wholes.
Focusing	Is the color relevant in this exercise?	No. The colored parts in the model are different than the colored parts in the frames below. The color is irrelevant.
Comparison and evaluation of different strategies	Shall we start from the top by an analysis of the whole, or from the bottom by a synthesis of the parts?	We had better start from the whole, since it is possible to put the same parts together in many different ways and get many new wholes (e.g., patchwork quilt).
Examples		Digits from 1 to 10 can be arranged in many different ways, but there is only one possible way to arrange them into a specific telephone number. Musical notes can be arranged in only one way for a specific tune.
Individuation and differentiation *Divergent response*		But if we categorize and describe the parts of the whole in the bottom frames, we can find a whole with the same components at the top of the page.
Regulation of behavior *Systematic work*	We will contrast the two starting points when you finish your independent work. After you have determined the starting point, what do you do?	The same as before. We describe the model by using categories—number and size. We look at all the possible answers until we find one that matches the description. We check to see if the answer has all the component parts.

MEDIATION OF:

Regulation of behavior; creating a set for future discussion	Why don't you work for a little while and then we can discuss the things you find helpful.	
Critical interpretation (Reference points)	*Independent work:* What have you discovered so far?	The number of parts is not helpful. They all have the same number.
Gathering information		The general class of figures is not very helpful. (On Page 8, the whole models all have triangles; on Page 9, they all have squares.)
Principle	**That which is common to many items cannot be used to differentiate among them.**	
	Examples: Looking up the name "Smith" in the telephone book; a uniform to differentiate among policemen.	
Transcendence		It is sometimes helpful to solve the easier problems first and thereby narrow the choices (e.g., test questions).
(Gathering information continued)		The third whole on Page 8 contains an arrowhead. Another has a tiny triangle.
Feeling of competence	You have found a part that is unique, one-of-a-kind. You are using a keystone to unlock the problem.	
Interpreting meaning of response		
Strategy for evaluation	How did you check your work?	By looking for the frames' components in the complete figure.
Principle—Meaning	**A whole can be identified by its elements.**	
Examples		An animal with a pouch, short forelegs, strong hind legs, and a long tail is a kangaroo.
Transcendence		

MEDIATION OF:

		Rhyme, meter, similes, and imagery define poetry. Seafood, tomato sauce, garlic and other spices, and rice make paella. Full description of height, weight, hair color, eye color, complexion, build, etc., identify a missing person.
Expansion of concept	Sometimes the dimensions of the elements remain unchanged in the process of their integration (e.g., a color-coordinated outfit).	
Examples	Sometimes there are changes in the characteristics of some of the elements. Can someone give us an example?	Two parts hydrogen and one part oxygen equals water. Vegetables and cream make up vegetable soup.
Discrimination		

Generalization	**The parts of a whole look very different in isolation from the way they appear embedded and integrated into the whole.**

Examples: Members of a family; staff workers; class members; pieces of a table before it is put together.

Discussion for insight	When do we look for the exceptional as a cue?	Temperature in a child indicated by flushed cheeks. Proofreading. Misprint in stamps and coins. The black pearl in the oyster. Weather that is different from the expected.
Transcendence		

Page 10

Objective

To correct the parts of a figure so that they agree with the figure's given components.

Subgoal

To be flexible in shifting from strategy to strategy.

Vocabulary

interchangeably   omission   commission

Mediation

Mediation of a feeling of competence is indicated in interpreting to the student the ways of identifying and correcting errors. Awareness of change is necessary for the student to perceive the difference between the model figure and the given components. Mediation of challenge may be required of the complex tasks in the third and fourth rows.

KEY TO THE FOLLOWING TEACHER-STUDENT INTERACTION

Rationale and analysis of teacher-student interaction	Teacher questions, comments, and activities (Notes to teacher)	Anticipated student responses; examples indicating mastery
	Teacher-student interaction of development of PRINCIPLES, CONCLUSIONS, SUMMARY STATEMENTS, and INSIGHT BY BRIDGING	

Page 10 (AV 4)

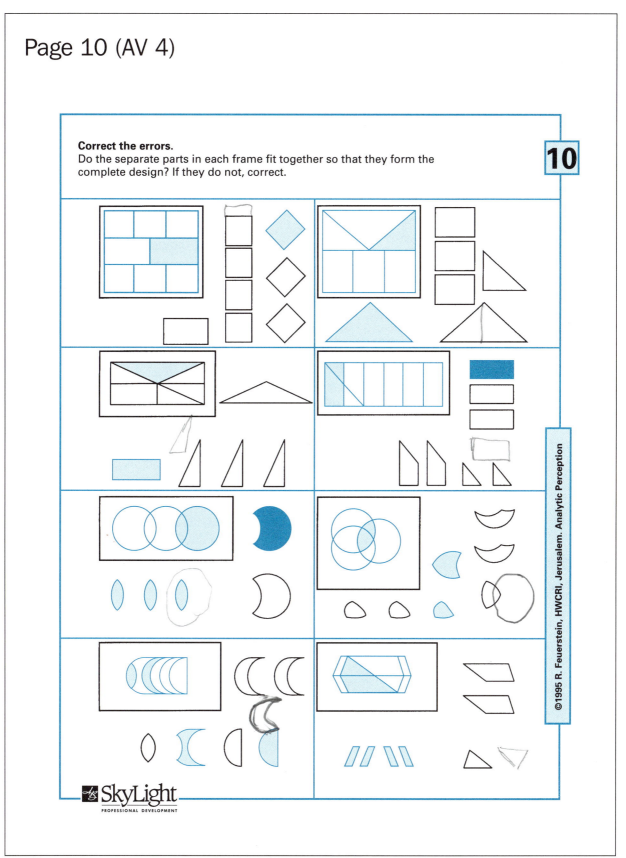

MEDIATION OF:

Decoding the instructions	Is all the necessary information given in the instructions?	No. It says, if it is wrong, correct. We don't know what we must correct from reading the instructions. It just says, correct. It doesn't tell us how.
Assuming responsibility		
	How will you know if there is an error?	We will follow the method we developed on Pages 8–9. If there are too many or too few parts, or not the right kind, we will know we have to correct the error.
	How will you correct the error?	It depends on the kind of error.
Meaning	**There can be many sources of an error. It is necessary to define an error in order to correct it.**	

Example: Evaluating a math or English paper vs. marking its errors.

Definition of task	Let's look at the first task. What do we see?	There is one more square than needed and one less rectangle.
Focus	How will you correct it?	We can mark out a square and draw a rectangle.
Interpreting to the student the meaning of his or her act	In other words, you are discarding what is not right and adding a whole new piece.	
Feeling of competence	Is that the only way to correct the problem?	No, we can add a piece to the extra square and make it a rectangle.
Insight	In other words, you are fixing what is wrong to make it appropriate. Can the two methods of correcting be used interchangeably?	
Feeling of competence		

MEDIATION OF:

Comparison	What happens if you spell a word wrong in a composition? Do you throw away the whole paper and write a new one?	No, we just change the word that was wrong. But if we cut a board too short, we can't add to it. We must put it aside and start again.
Hypothetical thinking		

Meaning

The method of correction must be appropriate to the needs of the task.

Throwing the incorrect part away is a drastic measure. It would be like expelling a person from school for chewing gum.

Independent work: (Both of the tasks in the third row and the first in the fourth row are extremely difficult because of their complexity and the difficulty in the representation of the isolated elements of the whole. One approach is to integrate the parts into new wholes [e.g., to analyze a circle into its segments, or a crescent into its component parts]. Another, more simplistic method, is to match parts on a one-to-one basis. An additional source of difficulty is the interference from the parts of the whole that are not being considered. In some instances it may be necessary to block out the irrelevant parts manually.)

Insight	What was the cause of your difficulties?	It was hard to picture the shape of the missing parts in the tasks in row 3.
Challenge		
Global perception	The tendency is the same as on Page 3—to see the figures globally. Here, we see circles and not the parts that together make a circle.	We had to keep changing the way we worked.
Feeling of competence	Yes, it was necessary to be flexible. We had to be willing to change when the situation changed.	

MEDIATION OF:

Transcendence | Can you give me some examples of an unexpected situation that results in a change in plans or actions? | Road detours; illness; unexpected expenses; goalie injured; electricity goes out; extra person for dinner.

Summary | **There are errors of omission and commission.**

Fostering a sense of completion

Future anticipation | We can forget to do something or we can do something wrong. We will discuss this again on later Pages of errors.

Teacher's Guide to Analytic Perception

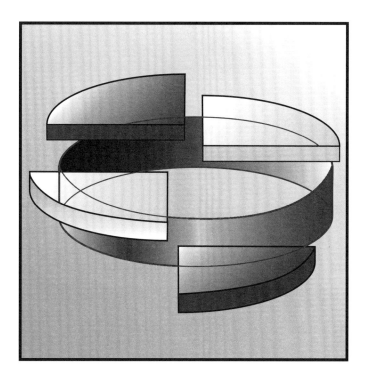

UNIT IV

Objectives

To understand that the synthesis of parts into a given whole is contingent upon a prior analysis of the whole into both its parts and the relationship between the parts.

To identify and describe those parts of a whole that are missing from the given component parts.

To construct the missing parts and to integrate them into those that are given so as to replicate the given model.

Subgoal

To use internal and external cues.

Pages 11–12

Analysis in Terms of the Cognitive Map

Content

Discrete elements and parts of parts to be integrated into a whole.

Modality

Figural.

Phase

Input

Precise and analytic perception of a whole that includes a description both of the parts and their relation to one another.

Use of spatial dimensions and directionality as attributes in localizing the position of given discrete parts within a whole and finding the spatial relationships between the parts.

Simultaneous use of several sources of information.

Use of temporal elements in sequencing.

Use of verbal labels to describe shapes, lines, orientation, and relationships.

Conserving the constancy of the parts of a whole despite superficial differences in their appearance.

Elaboration

Internalizing the model so as to be able to superimpose it on the given parts.

Spontaneous comparison of parts to the whole and to other parts.

Establishing and projecting relationships between the elements of the whole to one another and between the given parts to the given whole.

Selection of relevant cues.

Output

Use of visual transport.

Restraining impulsivity.

Operations

Closure of parts into a whole; articulation of the field; differentiation of a given model; representation of missing parts; identification of parts; integration of parts into a whole; construction.

Level of abstraction

Low.

Level of complexity

From low to high with some of the unfamiliar figures.

Level of efficiency

Can be brought up to high quickly.

Anticipated difficulties due to	Methods of eliminating, bypassing, or overcoming anticipated difficulties
Repetition of a line that is already given.	Breaking a part into its components. Erasing lines repeated in error. Use of verbal mediators to identify the precise parts that are missing.
Irregularity of drawn lines that mask the similarity of the figures.	Drawing the frame first. Using extrinsic cues when no intrinsic cues are given. (Drawing imaginary square around bottom figures on Page 12.)
Overlooking lines, orientation, or angles.	Interiorization of model figure, or its visual transport. With complex figures, analysis into smaller units.

Pages 11–12

NOTE: These two Pages are taught together.

Objective

To construct a figure similar to the model by an integration of discrete parts.

Vocabulary

frame	diagonal	identify	bisect
boundary	closure	dissimilarity	superimpose
discrete	internal cues	contrast	horizontal
internalize	external cues	intersect	vertical

Mediation

Mediation of feeling of competence is offered through approach and analysis of new tasks. Transcendence is mediated to aid in generalization of areas other than the tasks. Mediation of regulation and control of behavior is necessary to complete the figures accurately and precisely.

KEY TO THE FOLLOWING TEACHER-STUDENT INTERACTION

Rationale and analysis of teacher-student interaction	Teacher questions, comments, and activities (Notes to teacher)	Anticipated student responses; examples indicating mastery
	Teacher-student interaction of development of PRINCIPLES, CONCLUSIONS, SUMMARY STATEMENTS, and INSIGHT BY BRIDGING	

Page 11

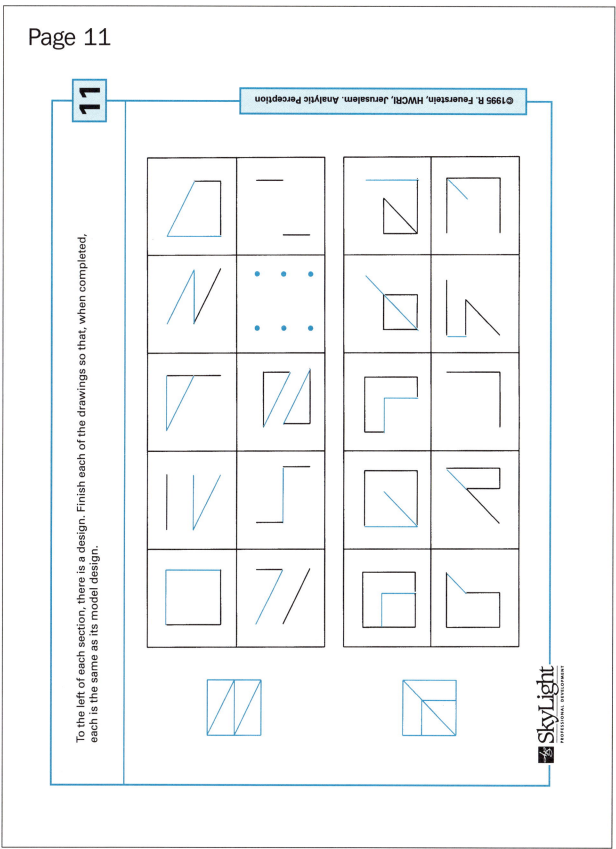

Page 12

©1995 R. Feuerstein, HWCRI, Jerusalem. Analytic Perception

To the left of each section you will find a design. Finish each of the drawings so that, when completed, each is the same as its model.

TEACHER'S GUIDE TO ANALYTIC PERCEPTION

MEDIATION OF:

Repetition and reinforcement of previously learned concepts	Before we start a new unit, let's review what we have learned until now in this instrument.	
	Who can tell us which two concepts are characteristic of the tasks in the first two units?	Analysis and synthesis.
Cognitive operation: verbal Definition of concepts	Very nice. What do these words mean?	Analysis is the breaking down of a whole and seeing what it's made of. Synthesis is putting together the parts in order to make a whole.
Bridging to indicate understanding: synthesis and analysis	Right. In the last unit we dealt with synthesis. Who has an example?	When one knits a sweater, one knits the parts separately and afterwards joins them. That's synthesis.
	Who has an example of analysis?	We analyze a story.
Transcendence	Can you explain what you mean?	We analyzed the story that we read. That means we broke the story into its parts to see how the author introduced the situation, built up to a climax, and resolved the situation. We also analyzed the characters and the relationships among them. We analyzed the part each played in the conflict.
	Very good. We had an example both of synthesis and analysis. Does anybody have another example?	In a laboratory they analyze blood to see if it contains all that a healthy person's blood should have. When one writes a sentence, one joins word to word in a synthesis. A composition is a synthesis of the introduction, the body, and the conclusion.

MEDIATION OF:

Feeling of competence by positive feedback and reinforcement	You have demonstrated that you all really understand the two concepts and can apply them to various situations.	
Request for generalization *Decoding instructions* *Use of spatial concepts* *Selection of stimuli*	Now look at the Page in front of you. Read the instructions and try to explain the task using the terms "synthesis" and "analysis."	We are given a whole on the left side of the Page. On the right side, parts of the whole are drawn and we have to complete them so the result will be the figure on the left side of the Page. Since not all of the parts are given in each frame, we have to look at the model to see what is missing.
	Right. Now try to express this in terms that are characteristic of this instrument.	We have to synthesize the parts.
(Positive verbal response to mediation)	Very nice. But is it only a synthesis?	In order to synthesize, first it is necessary to analyze the whole in order to know what it is made up of. Otherwise we won't know what is missing or how to join the various parts to make a whole.
Feeling of competence *Analytic perception of model* *Identification and description of verbal characteristics of model*	Excellent. Now let's analyze the whole figure. What is it made up of?	I can see two rectangles that were each divided into two triangles. I see a square with the letter Z inside of it. A square divided into four equal triangles with right angles.
Critical interpretation	Do you all agree with these analyses? Does anybody see anything wrong with these descriptions?	

MEDIATION OF:

Hypothetical thinking | What will happen if I put these four right-angled triangles next to each other so that each pair forms a rectangle? | You'll have double lines where the two triangles fit together. There will be two long sides of the triangle.

And this (pointing to the rectangles)? | The same thing. Double lines for the middle of the rectangle and for the triangles.

Precise definition | | I see a square with a line that is dividing it in half, and each half has a diagonal line from the upper left to the lower right.

Orientation as a dimension | Excellent. Perhaps you could just add the orientation of the bisecting line. | Horizontal.

Spatial orientation

Very good.

Meaning | **It is important to define the parts precisely to avoid error. Carefully studying the model simplifies the task of integrating its parts.**

Orientation to future | Excellent. Please start to work on the Page. I want to ask that while you are working you think about how you are solving each exercise.

Regulation of behavior

Independent work: (The students work independently while the teacher moves among them. Prior to discussion, the teacher draws one example from the Page on the board and asks students to complete it.)

MEDIATION OF:		
Problem-solving strategies	*Discussion:* How did you work?	I drew the frame first and then the diagonal line that was missing.
Seeking divergent response	Did anyone solve it another way?	I did. No, I didn't.
(Spontaneous correction); assuming responsibility	What was the matter?	I drew the diagonal in the wrong direction.
Sequencing temporal orientation; probe	Can you explain why you drew the frame first?	In order to know how far to draw the line.
(Function of frame) *Spontaneous comparison*	Good idea. What does the frame do?	It's like a border or a fence. It separates what is inside from what is outside. In social science, the teacher talks about frameworks. Is there any connection?
Regulation of behavior	Think about it for a moment while somebody looks in the dictionary.	
Definition of concept	(Write "border," "fence," "picture frame" in one list; "framework of society" in another list.)	The dictionary says a framework is a frame or structure composed of parts fitted and joined together.
Comparative behavior	What do all the words in the first list have in common?	We can see them and touch them. We can see what they enclose.
Critical interpretation	What about the second list?	It is one kind of frame but we cannot touch it or see the things it encloses.
Meaning; identification and description: verbal	**We have frames that can be seen, touched, and felt. They are concrete. There are also frames we know about but cannot really see or touch. They are abstract.**	

MEDIATION OF:

Discussion for insight

Meaning

We said that a frame limits. Is there any advantage to limits and borders?

Our country has a border. Only people who meet certain requirements are let into the country.

Association and application

What about on this Page?

In this case, we couldn't do the task without them.

Generalization

In other areas?

They help organize.

Transcendence

Like the example in Comparisons when we drew a circle around fruit. The circle was the border to keep all the fruit together.

Discrimination

That's one way the limit is good. But it also keeps things out (e.g., No _____ Allowed), and sometimes that's not good.

That's a very interesting comment. Let's summarize. What did you learn today?

Fostering a sense of completion

We learned to connect separate things in a certain way to construct a figure similar to that in the model. We learned that it is necessary to limit a task before we start.

Repetition

In our last lesson we spoke of frames and frameworks as limits.

Instructions as limits

Are there any limits to these tasks?

We must complete the frames so they are exactly like the model.

Problem-solving strategies

Practically speaking, what does that mean?

We must analyze the model to see what it is made of and compare it with the frames to see what parts are missing. Then we must build the whole from the independent parts in a synthesis.

Operational definition of task

Analysis and synthesis

MEDIATION OF:

Probe	You said "analyze." Do we just look at the parts?	
Meaning	**If the figure is simple, it is possible to transport it visually, or through seeing it in our mind.** **If the figure is complex, we must label the parts and their relationship to each other.**	
Seeking differences; definition of process of contrasting; comparison; differentiation	Contrast the task on the top of Page 12 with that on the bottom. Before we contrast what must we do?	Look at each separately to see exactly what it is. Then compare them to each other to see how they differ; then pick out the most important results of our comparison to discuss.
Using several sources of information Identification and description of task: verbal	What information have you gathered?	The model figure in the first task is a triangle. Each angle has a line that bisects it (divides it exactly in half). The three lines are continued only to the point of intersection. A cue to that point is given in each of the tasks. The figure in the bottom doesn't have a universal label. There are two figures that look like rectangles with curved ends that cross each other diagonally. The place they intersect is a square that is diagonal to the bottom of the page.
Developing inferential thinking; inference	What conclusion can you reach as a result of contrasting the two?	The bottom will be more difficult to do.
Probe Logical evidence	Why?	The triangle has enough cues to allow us to draw the frame, and to be precise in drawing the lines that meet. In the bottom task there are no intrinsic cues of

MEDIATION OF:

		angles and sides. We will have to draw an imaginary square very lightly around the figure to keep the arms the same length.
Conclusion	**When there are no cues given, it is necessary to create our own reference points.**	
Divergent responses	Is it necessary to keep looking at the model figure?	Yes, to be sure we are right.
Critical interpretation		No. If we describe the model correctly to ourselves or if we have a picture of it in our imagination, we don't have to look at it all the time. We know what our flag looks like without having it in front of us.
Fostering independence	How will we check our work?	If the completed figure looks the same in all details, it is correct.
Competence	You are speaking of being given immediate feedback by the task. Do you have any examples?	If I work my combination lock right, it opens. If not, it doesn't.
Transcendence		If I don't put enough change in the vending machine, my selection does not come out.

Critical interpretation

Various subjects for discussion in completing Pages 11 and 12:
1. The easiest models to replicate are those closest to something we already know or those that are divided according to a logical pattern or order (squares or triangles).
2. It is necessary to have cues or reference points to reconstruct a whole. Descriptions such as "bisect," "parallel," "median," and "intersect" are helpful.
3. There is a resemblance of some of the tasks to Organization of Dots, in which we had to draw an imaginary line to form the relationship between two dots.
4. It is possible to reconstruct a whole from different given parts as long as there is a model.

5. Although each contains elements of the same whole, the frames are very dissimilar. It is hard to see a superficial relationship between them. The relationship becomes apparent only as a result of investment on our part.
6. The resemblance of some of the frames to the whole is more obvious when the parts that are given are critical or when the connection between them is more obvious.
7. There are many instances when we must identify what is missing to make a whole identical to our model of it (e.g., seasoning from the soup; the setting of a table; filling in an outline map; students absent from class; unanswered question on a test).

Teacher's Guide to Analytic Perception

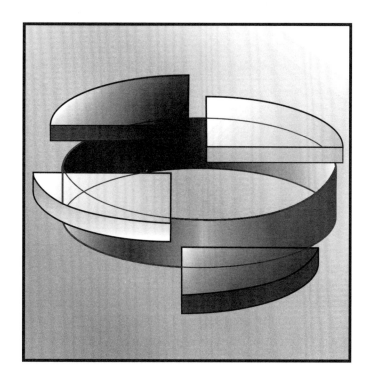

UNIT V

Objective

To integrate the complementary parts into a given whole.

Pages 13–17

Analysis in Terms of the Cognitive Map

Content

Parts that are themselves components of parts.

Modality

Figural, with verbal instructions, and letter and number codes.

Phase

Input

Analytic perception with a differentiation of the whole into its component parts and an integration of parts into a new whole.

Precise perception of internal and external lines.

Labeling precisely the parts of the whole and their relation to one another.

Use of a code to specify specific figures.

Use of two sources in the construction of the whole.

Use of spatial dimension to describe parts and their relationships.

Conservation of constancy of components over changes in their setting and context.

Systematic exploration and systematic work in marking off those items that have already been used.

Elaboration

Spontaneous comparison of new whole to the model to determine those elements that are missing.

Comparison of the content of each frame to a verbal description of what is missing.

Establishment and projection of the relationships through which two wholes will be integrated into a figure identical to the model.

Use of hypothetical thinking and logic in the representational joining of two complementary parts.

Broadened psychological field to bear in mind both the given parts and those that are represented.

Increased use of visual transport by which the model is mentally superimposed over one of the given parts in an attempt to define the characteristics of its complementary parts.

Output

Need for precision and accuracy in responses.

Deferring responses until hypothesis has been tested representationally.

Restraint of impulsivity.

Operations

Differentiation and integration; closure; representation; anticipation; inferential thinking; deductive and inductive reasoning.

Level of abstraction

High since the task is solved through representation and the answer is encoded in letters and numbers.

Level of complexity

Very high since figures are not familiar and are composed of many parts.

Level of efficiency

Relatively low.

Anticipated difficulties due to	Methods of eliminating, bypassing, or overcoming anticipated difficulties
Improper definition of model so that it is impossible to find complementary parts. (If the model on Page 17 is described as nine squares, it is impossible to find three squares to complete the six that are given.)	Break down the parts of the whole into their parts in the description of labeling of the whole. (Instead of nine squares, say one square with two horizontal and two vertical lines that intersect at equal distances.)
Global perception of whole.	Use of summative behavior (three radii, not some radii).
Blocking.	Allow student to complete task by construction, as for Pages 11 and 12. Then give student fresh Page to solve representationally.
Selecting parts that repeat given lines or lack complements.	Overcome impulsivity by hypothetical thinking and anticipation of sought part.

Pages 13–17

NOTE: Page 16 is an Error Page and may be taught at the end of this unit.

Objectives

To complete a model representationally by joining two complementary parts, each of which is a whole composed of several parts.

To identify parts that are missing from a whole and to recognize them in a new setting.

Subgoal

To practice differentiation and integration.

Vocabulary

radius	common lines	complete	circumference
midpoint	internal lines	complement	perimeter
intersection	external lines	assembly	segment

Mediation

Mediation of challenge is elicited in these Pages by the novelty and complexity of the tasks. Mediation of a feeling of competence may be necessary by more adequately preparing students for these Pages by reviewing Pages 11 and 12 and interpreting to students the reasons for their difficulties. Mediation of intentionality, reciprocity, transcendence, and meaning is indicated by summarizing the unit.

KEY TO THE FOLLOWING TEACHER-STUDENT INTERACTION

Rationale and analysis of teacher-student interaction	Teacher questions, comments, and activities (Notes to teacher)	Anticipated student responses; examples indicating mastery
	Teacher-student interaction of development of PRINCIPLES, CONCLUSIONS, SUMMARY STATEMENTS, and INSIGHT BY BRIDGING	

MEDIATION OF:

Page 13

Comparison and recall *Goal-seeking behavior*	How do the tasks on this Page differ from those on the previous Pages?	In the previous unit we completed the whole by drawing in the parts that were missing. Here, we have to find two parts (one from the left column and one from the right column) that we can put together in our imagination (by representation).
Identification and description	We are looking for two complementary parts. (On board.) Let's look at the first task. Why are A and 4 complementary parts? What was missing from A?	(From dictionary) An addition that completes. One line. One radius. The middle radius and the midpoint.
Hypothetical thinking	What would have happened if you had merely defined the missing part as a radius?	We wouldn't have found it because there is no such thing given.
Meaning	**We must precisely and completely define exactly what we are looking for in order to find it.**	
Cognitive operation (mental superimposition of part transported visually)	Imagine 4 placed on A. Is the result the same as the model? Is it necessary to draw it in?	Yes. No. We can see it in our mind's eye.
Challenge: novelty and complexity	If there are no questions, please start to work.	

Independent work: (Students who have great difficulty in representation can be allowed to draw in the lines lightly or by finger tracing. However, the Page should then be reworked "in the mind," using verbal descriptions. Another method is to draw the figure completed through representation on a piece of scratch paper.)

Page 13

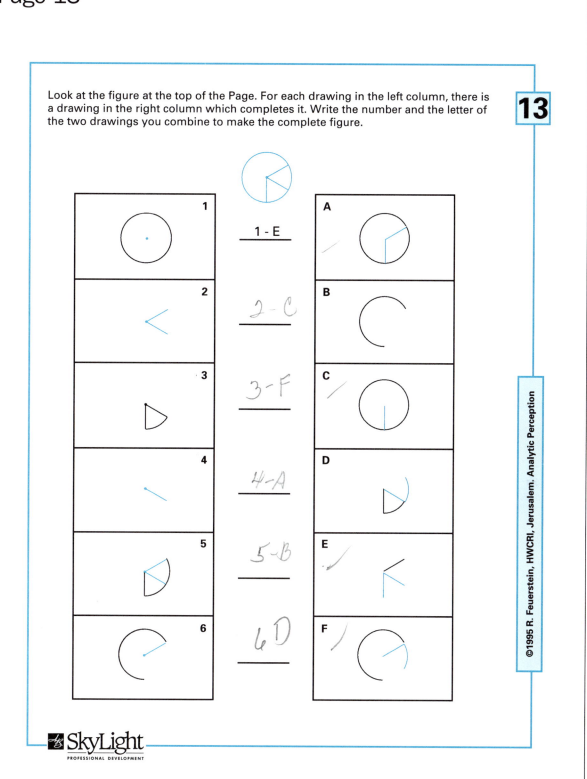

MEDIATION OF:

Discrimination; directing attention to synthesis of two parts	*Discussion:* Why was 2 not the complement of B?	Because if we put them together, the middle radius and a portion of the perimeter would be missing.
Meaning	**One must look at both the internal and external lines to identify what is missing.**	
Immediate feedback; problem-solving strategies	What can we do that will help us to be sure we have solved the Page correctly?	We can check off the letters and numbers as soon as we use them. If we are correct, the last pair should be complementary.

Page 14

Critical interpretation	The whole must be labeled properly. If it is defined as a triangle with two small triangles, there will be an immediate error in complementing A, which is described as a triangle. From the definition, two small triangles are missing. #1 matches that definition. However, if #1 is used, there is a repetition of outside lines. The internal lines should be defined as a V or better still, as one vertical and one diagonal line.
Meaning	**It is necessary to break even a part into its elements.**

Page 14

Look at the figure at the top of the Page. For each drawing in the left column, there is a drawing in the right column which completes it. Write the number and the letter of the two drawings you combine to make the complete figure.

1 — A

Page 15

MEDIATION OF:

Identification and description: verbal

The model figure and its components must be relabeled and redefined from task to task:
Two overlapping hearts pointing in opposite directions, connected by a vertical line.
Two ellipses diagonally superimposed with a vertical line connecting two points of intersection.
A flower with four petals and a vertical line in the rounded square of its center.

Meaning

The parts of a whole appear different when they are taken out of context and isolated.

Summary

In order to check one's work one can reverse the procedure. Instead of finding a complement to the part on the right side, find those that complement the parts on the left side of the Page.

The whole is drawn with two different colors as are each of the drawings that complement each other, but there is no consistency in this division of color. This imposes an irrelevant source of information on the perceptual process. Students have to recognize the answers despite change in color.

Page 15

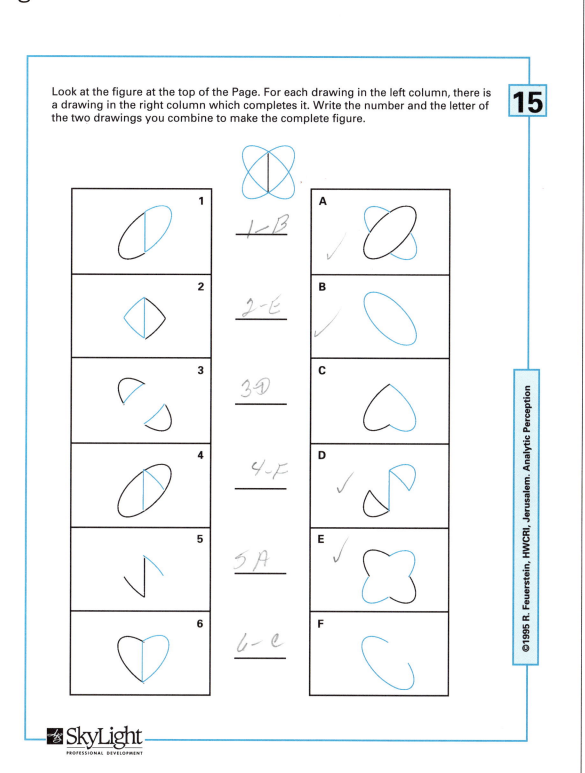

Page 16

MEDIATION OF:

Need for logical evidence (input levels) — Either the letter or number can be corrected, but not both. What will be changed is a function of which figure from which column is being completed. The corrected answers will be the same, no matter which is the referent, but will appear in different places on the Page.

Meaning — **To make a correction, one must know why the given answer is wrong, and either add or subtract.**

Page 16

Correct the errors.
Look at the figure at the top of the page. Each drawing on the left, when combined with a drawing on the right will form the figure at the top of the page. You are to correct the answers by changing the letters or numbers so that the correct combinations are listed.

16

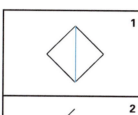

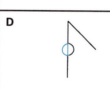

1 - D
2 - C
3 - E
4 - F
5 - A
6 - B

© 1995 R. Feuerstein, HWCRI, Jerusalem. Analytic Perception

Page 17

MEDIATION OF:

Challenge: complexity

Since the tasks in the unit increase in complexity, this Page is the most difficult. The model demonstrates the synthesis of parts into an integrated whole. To be aware of its components, one must break it into its elements. The elements and their relationships to one another determine the whole that is far more than the sum of its parts.

Transcendence

Topics for discussion and/or insight:
Complements: Given the quotient and the multiplicand, one can deduce what is missing.
One sews the bodice, back, collar, and sleeves into a blouse; one sews the back and front pieces together into a skirt. The two wholes, each composed of parts, are parts of a greater whole. They are the complementary parts of a dress.
A carburetor is composed of many parts. It, in turn, is a complementary part of the car's combustion system.
In baking a cake, the solids and the liquids are mixed separately, and then united to form the whole batter.

Context: It is not elevation alone that makes a mountain high, but also the elevation of the land surrounding it.
Behaviors must be judged within the context in which they occur. Formal language and slang (e.g., contractions are not used in a formal composition).
Digits have different values in different positions.

Correction of errors: Knowing the source of an error may not always lead to its correction. However, it is certain that an error that is not identified cannot be corrected.

A whole is more than the sum of its parts: A building is more than an assortment of wood, plaster, nails, glass, wire, etc.

Page 17 (AV 5)

Look at the figure at the top of the Page. For each drawing in the left column, there is a drawing in the right column which completes it. Write the number and the letter of the two drawings you combine to make the complete figure.

1. D
2. A
3. E
4. F
5. B
6. C

Teacher's Guide to Analytic Perception

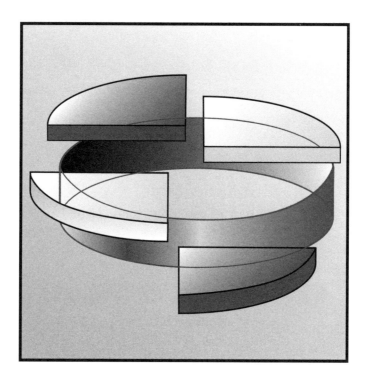

UNIT VI

Objective

To unite discrete parts into a whole.

Pages 18–20

Analysis in Terms of the Cognitive Map

Content

Part-whole relationships.

Modality

Figural, with verbal instructions, and a cipher to signify parts.

Phase

Input

Precise perception of the shape and size of parts and their angles, and the orientation of external lines.

Labeling of attributes of the part.

Conservation of constancy of elements of a whole despite apparent transformations that result from their assemblage.

Systematic search and scanning.

Use of several sources of information.

Using a code to identify parts.

Elaboration

Establishing the relationship among the elements that are assembled into the whole.

Internalization of figure.

Output

Precise communication of response.

Operations

Identification; integration; disembedding; hypothetical thinking.

Level of abstraction

Low.

Level of complexity

Rises with successive Pages.

Level of efficiency

Initially low; rises with successive Pages.

Anticipated difficulties due to	Methods of eliminating, bypassing, or overcoming anticipated difficulties
Mistaking parts similar in shape but different in the orientation of their external lines.	Investment in perceiving and describing attributes of the items, and the directionality of lines.
Difficulty in moving from the concrete task to more abstract applications.	Working together to discover the principle and applying the principle to a variety of areas.

Pages 18–20

Objectives

To understand that parts that are wholes can be combined to form new wholes.

To identify the components of the new wholes and the relationship of the parts to one another.

To be aware that the merger between two parts erases their internal boundaries.

Subgoal

To use a cipher to designate a part.

Vocabulary

compound   merger   solution   fusion

Mediation

Mediation of awareness of change in differentiating between current tasks and those in earlier Pages and in differentiating parts of the whole. Intentionality, reciprocity, transcendence, and meaning should be emphasized in this unit in which new concepts are introduced. Mediation of regulation and control of behavior is elicited in the need to focus and attend to fine differences of size, orientation, and location.

KEY TO THE FOLLOWING TEACHER-STUDENT INTERACTION

Rationale and analysis of teacher-student interaction	Teacher questions, comments, and activities (Notes to teacher)	Anticipated student responses; examples indicating mastery
	Teacher-student interaction of development of PRINCIPLES, CONCLUSIONS, SUMMARY STATEMENTS, and INSIGHT BY BRIDGING	

Page 18

Comparison *Seeking differences*	Look at Page 3. How do the tasks on this Page differ from those on Page 3?	There, the direction of the parts didn't matter. Here, it does.
Principle	**In many instances, directionality is a critical attribute.**	
Transcendence by example		In distinguishing between b and d, p and q, and + and ×. Upstream and downstream. The direction a refrigerator door opens.
Differentiation (gathering complete information)	Are there any other differences between the Pages?	On Page 3, the parts were single pieces hidden in the whole. Here, the parts are made up of more than one piece.
Problem-solving strategies	Will the fact that several pieces have been united into one part make any difference in your solution of the task?	We must ignore the lines between the parts. For example, on the top of the Page it is difficult to see that the middle whole in the first row is made up of 2, 3, and 5, since the concave lines of 2 and 3 disappear the minute we add 5.
Meaning	**The lines separating two parts are erased in a merger between them.**	
Transcendence	*Examples:* Two companies join into one; red and yellow combine to make orange; fat and alkali make soap; team play as opposed to solo performance.	

Page 18

Each section which appears below the given design is composed of a number of parts. On the line beneath each section, write the numbers of the parts it contains.

18

4-3

6-2-3

1-5

4-5,2

1-4-3

1-2-3-4-5

2-3

1-4

4-3

4-2-1

1-2

2-4-3

MEDIATION OF:

Differentiation: compound solution		Sometimes they can be separated again without injuring the parts: salad dressing will separate into oil and water and vinegar.
Transcendence		A mixed bouquet of autumn flowers can be divided back into dahlias and chrysanthemums, and so on.
Similarity	On the bottom of Page 18, and on Pages 19 and 20, the orientation of angles and protuberances is the key to locating the parts.	We will have to pay attention to shape, size, and direction of the lines. For instance, in the bottom task on Page 18, piece 2 looks like pieces 3 and 4 combined except for the orientation of the lines.
Reciprocity		Here, the new part must appear in exactly the same orientation as in the model. There are no reversals or turns.

Meaning	**The orientation of the part relative to the whole in which it is found must be conserved.**

Examples	The right sleeve goes into the right armhole.
Transcendence	The adjective precedes the noun. A motor must be assembled with each of its parts in a specific location relative to the others. In math equations in which there is subtraction or division, the location of elements relative to each other must be preserved.

Independent work: Page 18, bottom, first row, right: sometimes students confuse part 2 with parts 3 and 4.

Page 19

Each of the models is divided into seven parts. (Refer to the discussion of greater complexity with greater number of parts.) The task at bottom of the Page is difficult because the parts are small; 4, 5, and 6 are identical in size but not in location; 1, 2, 6, and 4, and 2, 3, 6, and 5 are identical so additional cues must be used to determine the given.

MEDIATION OF:

Intentionality

Discussion: In these Pages we spoke of wholes that were integrated from the separate parts and the identification of the parts of a larger whole that were integrated.

Transcendence

Let us take two examples of new wholes made of individual parts; the violin section in an orchestra, and concrete used in building.

The violin section can be separated back into individual violinists; the concrete cannot be separated into sand, gravel, and water without destroying the concrete.

This is similar in some ways to the sets we learned about in Comparisons. Let's take fruit. Can it be divided?

Fruit is similar to the orchestra. We can pull out apples and oranges, and put them back again without destroying the set.

What is an example of sets that are destroyed when we remove one or another of their components?

Creative Writing. We can't remove either the Creative or the Writing without destroying the class.

Meaning

The new whole may have new characteristics that result from the fusion of its parts.

Page 19 (AV 6)

Each section which appears below the given design is composed of a number of parts. On the line beneath each section, write the numbers of the parts it contains.

19

1-2-3   2-3   3-4-6   3-4

2-3-4-5   1-2-3-4-5   2-3-4-5-6   4-5

2-6   6-5   1-2-6-4-5-7   1-4-7

1-2-3-4-5-6   2-3   3-5   4-5-7

MEDIATION OF:

Examples Oil and vinegar are liquids. When you shake them up, the liquid gets thick.

Transcendence Red and blue become purple.

MEDIATION OF:

Page 20

Anticipated intentionality (definition of problem)	What are we supposed to do on this Page?	We must see whether the numbers under the part merge into the whole. If they do, we mark the task with a + and go on. If they don't, we put a – in the circle.
Reciprocity (problem-solving strategy)		Then we find the parts that correctly compose the whole that is given and write the numbers on the line.
Modeling		6, 7, 10, and 11 are given as numbers for the trapezoid. We look at the whole for numbers 6, 7, 10, and 11. They form a trapezoid like the one below, so we put a + in the given circle.
Repetition	When we correct, is it necessary to cross out all the given numbers?	No. As in other tasks, we only change what is wrong. We can insert missing numbers, cross out extra numbers, and change incorrect numbers.
Confrontation with reality (exploration of alternatives)	Would there be another way to correct the error?	We could change the drawing so it corresponds to the given numbers. But that is not acceptable in this task because of the instructions given.

Page 20

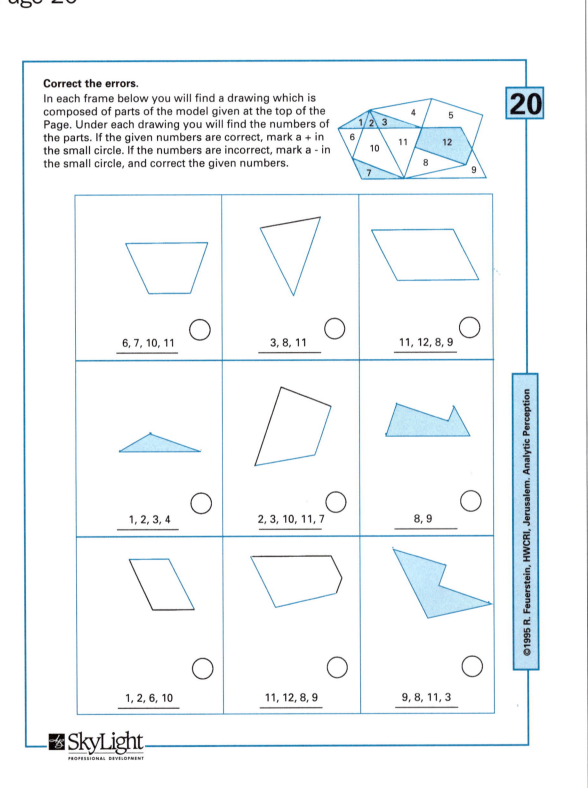

Teacher's Guide to Analytic Perception

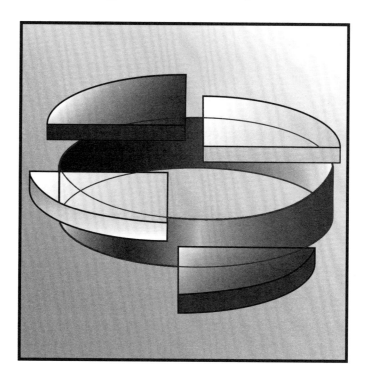

UNIT VII

Objective

To isolate a composite that is embedded in a complex whole.

Subgoal

To develop an awareness for the need for precision.

Pages 21–22

Analysis in Terms of the Cognitive Map

Content

Composite and complex wholes.

Modality

Graphic and figural.

Phase

Input

Precise perception of the composite whole with attention to fine detail.

Use of verbal labels to describe shape, size, and orientation.

Use of spatial orientation as a dimension.

Conservation of constancy of figure over changes stemming from being embedded in a complex whole.

Use of several sources of information in the search.

Systematic search and scanning.

Elaboration

Comparison to model.

Use of relevant cues in absence of an external frame of reference.

Internalization of composite.

Output

Restraint of impulsivity.

Operations

Articulation of field; segregation; integration; differentiation.

Level of abstraction

Low.

Level of complexity

High.

Level of efficiency

Medium.

Anticipated difficulties due to	Methods of eliminating, bypassing, or overcoming anticipated difficulties
Inability to determine where the composite is in the complex whole.	Select as a reference point a detail (a protuberance, an angle, a line) and try to locate it in the whole. With one finger, trace the shape of the composite, while with the other hand, draw the line that is being traced as it appears in the whole.
Deciding between two figures, both of which seem correct.	Student discussion in which two responses are equally appropriate, and reasons for decision.

Pages 21–22

Objectives

To isolate a composite that is embedded in a complex whole.

To identify and delineate the parts in the whole.

To review previously acquired learning.

Subgoal

To ignore the distraction of irrelevant information.

Mediation

Mediation of feeling of competence in reviewing previous learning. Mediation of regulation and control of behavior as necessary to differentiate between parts that are similar in form, size, and orientation.

KEY TO THE FOLLOWING TEACHER-STUDENT INTERACTION

Rationale and analysis of teacher-student interaction	Teacher questions, comments, and activities (Notes to teacher)	Anticipated student responses; examples indicating mastery
	Teacher-student interaction of development of PRINCIPLES, CONCLUSIONS, SUMMARY STATEMENTS, and INSIGHT BY BRIDGING	

127 TEACHER'S GUIDE TO ANALYTIC PERCEPTION

MEDIATION OF:

Repetition

In this unit we will review many of the things we've already done.

Regulation of behavior

Please look at the task for a few minutes and then we will list what we are reviewing.

NOTE: Necessity of reading and understanding instructions to decide what we are to do and how we will plan our work.

Problem-solving strategies

What do we have to do?

We must look at the composite in Row A and find it in Row B. When we have found it, we color it.

Feeling of competence

That sounds easy. Is it?

No, because the composite is hidden in a figure with lots of lines.

We must look at the composite carefully and label it. We must describe its characteristics and pick the cues that will help us. When we think we have found what we are looking for, we compare it to the model.
If it is not correct, we see what is wrong, and use that information to guide us.
If it is correct, we color it.

Independent work:
Page 21: Figure 2 in row B at bottom of page has two correct answers.
Page 22: Parts are similarly shaped so task requires fine discrimination.

Page 21

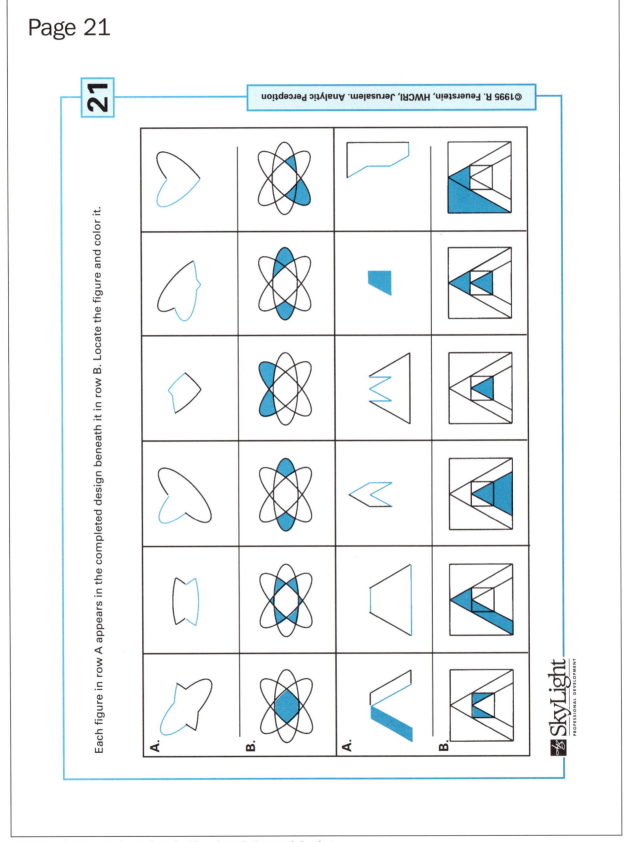

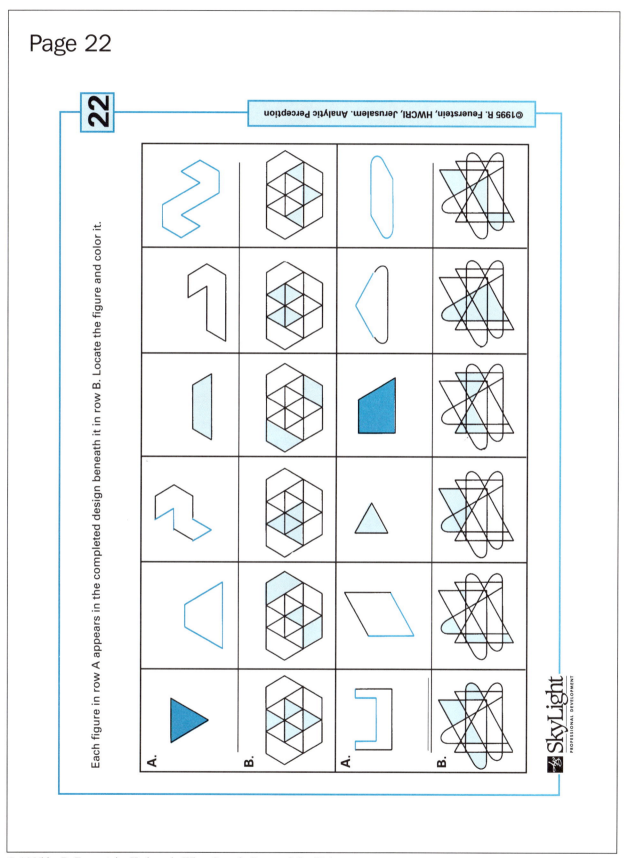

MEDIATION OF:

Summary | *Discussion for insight and/or bridging:* Can we summarize what we are learning in a few sentences?

Meaning | **A whole object may be composed of many parts that themselves are wholes. It in turn may be a part of another whole that includes it.**

Transcendence for application of principle | An airplane is a complex whole, but each of its parts (engines, ailerons, wings, landing gear, etc.) is a whole in itself. Each part, too, is composed of many parts.
A chapter in a book.
France as a composite of many areas.
Lungs as a part of the respiratory system.

Meaning | **There is more than one correct answer in some situations.**

Examples: Planning a menu to include basic food elements; choosing what to wear; $5 = 1+1+1+1+1$ or $2+3$ or $2+2+1$ or $1\frac{1}{2}+1\frac{1}{2}+2$ or $3+2$ or $1+2+2$ or $2+1+2$.

Transcendence | There are instances in which one thing can simultaneously be part of or belong to two or more others. However, it can only be *used* with one at any one time. | *Example:* My sister and I share a sweater. Only one of us can wear it at any one time.
I share a compass and protractor with a friend. We have to decide who is going to do their math homework first.

Teacher's Guide to Analytic Perception

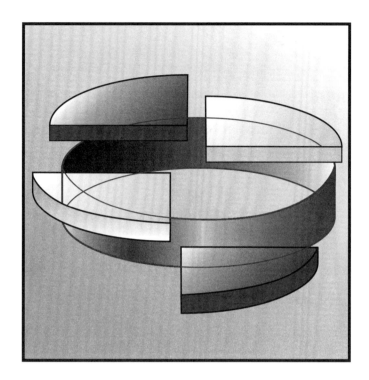

UNIT VII

Objectives

To construct a whole from identifiable parts.

To learn that only certain components will make a specific whole.

Pages 23–25

Analysis in Terms of the Cognitive Map

Content

Frame for the construction of composites.

Modality

Figural, with verbal instructions, and the use of a number code.

Phase

Input

Translation of code into appropriate figures.

Perception of attributes of given parts.

Use of several sources of information.

Conservation of constancy of figure, despite changes in its location.

Elaboration

Internalization of figure.

Establishment of the relationships among the parts.

Comparison of completed figures to model.

Selection of relevant cues.

Output

Visual transport of given part.

Construction only after integration of parts into a whole.

Operations

Identification; representation; integration; differentiation.

Level of abstraction

Low.

Level of complexity

Medium to high.

Level of efficency

Initially low; rises with successive Pages.

Anticipated difficulties due to	Methods of eliminating, bypassing, or overcoming anticipated difficulties
Drawing the internal lines between the component parts.	Rereading of instructions. Review of reason why internal lines are superfluous.
Problem of estimating distance when reference points are not given.	Teaching students how to project imaginary lines to divide a whole area into its parts.
Constructing figures that do not touch other lines.	Using aids when precision is critical.

Pages 23–25

Objectives

To construct new wholes from identifiable parts.

To summarize instrument.

Subgoal

To establish reference points.

Mediation

Goal-seeking, goal-planning, and goal-achieving behavior is mediated in tasks that differ from Page to Page and within the Pages themselves. Mediation for a feeling of competence may be necessary in interpreting to students the meaning of their activities and the application of these activities to other areas. Sharing behavior is evident in the examples of bridging for transcendence.

KEY TO THE FOLLOWING TEACHER-STUDENT INTERACTION

Rationale and analysis of teacher-student interaction	Teacher questions, comments, and activities (Notes to teacher)	Anticipated student responses; examples indicating mastery
	Teacher-student interaction of development of PRINCIPLES, CONCLUSIONS, SUMMARY STATEMENTS, and INSIGHT BY BRIDGING	

MEDIATION OF:

Page 23

Assuming responsibility by paraphrasing instruction	Please define the task in your own words.	In the dotted figure we are supposed to draw the figure that is made up of the parts whose numbers are given. Only the outline of the new figure is drawn.
Probe; directing attention	What do you learn from the completed example?	That we are supposed to darken the outside lines that belong to the figure we draw.
Deductive reasoning	Why is that necessary?	Otherwise we wouldn't know which was part 2 and 3, and which was part 1 and 4.
Comparative behavior	What is the difference between the givens on the top of the Page and those on the bottom?	A dot has been given as a point of reference for the triangle but not for the trapezoid.
Intentionality	**When we are not given a reference point, we must construct one.**	

Page 23

In each of the following outlines you are to draw the section that is composed of the parts whose numbers appear beneath the outline. Pay attention. Do not include the lines between the parts you draw.

Pages 24–25

MEDIATION OF:

Use of frames of reference

Page 24: The diagonal of the rectangle provides a frame of reference for the side of the trapezoid (part #1). The vertical line that bisects the rectangle also helps by providing a reference point for the other lines. Draw imaginary lines to divide the whole into quarters and thirds before you draw the actual lines.

Page 25: Two reference points are given since the division does not utilize easily projected divisions.

Focus and selection of stimuli

Transcendence

In these Pages, it is clear that we are only interested in one part, complex though it may be, of the whole. The other parts do not interest us.

Examples: Building inspectors differ for electrical work, plumbing, and construction codes. Separate grades for content/neatness, spelling, and grammar in compositions.

Logical reasoning

Problem-solving strategies

Were there any strategies that contributed to your efficiency?

When all the numbers were given, I knew that I had to draw only the outside line.
When all but one number were given, it was easier to mark the missing part and eliminate it.

Comparative behavior

Please contrast these tasks with those on Pages 18–22.

On Pages 18–22, the part was already drawn for us. All we had to do was to identify the numbers of the parts of the whole that made up the part in question. Here we do the reverse. We construct a part from the subpart numbers provided.

Meaning

It is easier to recognize something than it is to construct it.

MEDIATION OF:

Transcendence

Examples: It is easier to understand a foreign language than to speak it; it is easier to recognize the Empire State Building than to build it.

Subjects for discussion for insight and/or bridging:
Construction of reference points in daily experiences.
Summary and review of what was learned in Analytic Perception:
- A summary sentence should be composed for the main principle of each unit.
- Review of some of the main principles discussed.
- Application of the principles mentioned to academic and vocational subjects and life experiences.

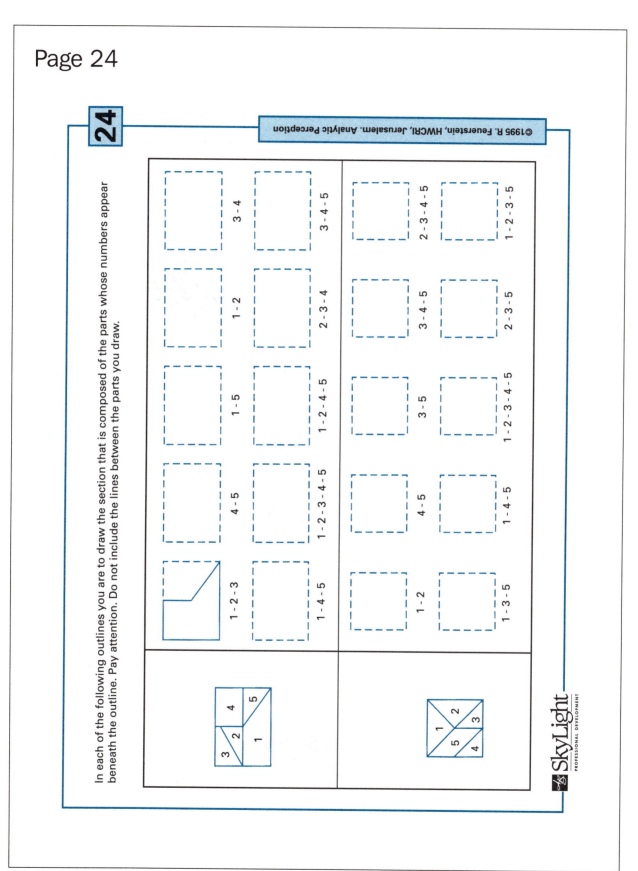

Page 25 (AV 7)